ROAD MAP FOR REVOLUTIONARIES

ROAD
REVOLUT

* * * * * * * * * * * * * *

RESISTANCE
ADVOCACY

MAP FOR
ONARIES

FOR

ACTIVISM AND

FOR ALL

ELISA CAMAHORT PAGE
CAROLYN GERIN
JAMIA WILSON

ILLUSTRATIONS BY
JOSH MACPHEE

INFOGRAPHICS BY
LILLI KEINAENEN

TEN SPEED PRESS

California | New York

Check out **roadmapforrevolutionaries.com** for chapter notes, additional material, news and updates, recommendations for further reading, author speaking engagements, meet-ups, and more.

Published in the United States by Ten Speed Press, an imprint of the Crown Publishing Group, a division of Penguin Random House LLC, New York.
www.crownpublishing.com
www.tenspeed.com

Ten Speed Press and the Ten Speed Press colophon are registered trademarks of Penguin Random House LLC.

A portion of chapter 1 is adapted from "Allied Force: A guide to Showing up Without Getting in the Way" by Jamia Wilson (*Rookie*, 1/14/15).

Trade Paperback ISBN: 978-0-399-58164-9
eBook ISBN: 978-0-399-58165-6

Printed in China

Design by Debbie Berne

10 9 8 7 6 5 4 3 2 1

First Edition

Library of Congress Cataloging-in-Publication Data

Names: Camahort Page, Elisa, author. | Gerin, Carolyn, author. | Wilson, Jamia, 1980- author.
Title: Road map for revolutionaries: resistance, activism, and advocacy for all / Elisa Camahort Page, Carolyn Gerin, and Jamia Wilson ; illustrations by Josh MacPhee; infographics by Lilli Keinaenen.
Description: First edition. | California: Ten Speed Press, 2018. | Includes bibliographical references and index.
Identifiers: LCCN 2017053992|
Subjects: LCSH: Civil disobedience—United States. | Protest movements—United States. | Social advocacy—United States. | BISAC: POLITICAL SCIENCE / Political Process / Political Advocacy. | POLITICAL SCIENCE / Political Process / Elections.
Classification: LCC JC328.3 .G475 2018 | DDC 322.4/20973—dc23
LC record available at https://lccn.loc.gov/2017053992

To friends, family, neighbors, and colleagues
who are at our sides, raising their voices, and
rolling up their sleeves, whether lifelong activists
or newly fired up. We're in this together!

CONTENTS

2 PROTECTING YOURSELF ONLINE AND OFF

41

3 ECONOMIC PRESSURE

67

"Struggle is a never-ending process. Freedom is never really won, you earn it and win it in every generation."
—Coretta Scott King

Every activist has a story. Every part-time revolutionary has a defining moment. Before they grabbed the megaphone, made their first protest sign, or put pen to paper. Before they rallied their communities or took a lonely stand. These are the moments when they realized that they could change the world. Let their stories inspire your story.

"As a marketer, I had spent my entire career working with young people, helping them find the latest sneakers, best-tasting drinks, and fastest cars. But in 2008, I was asked by the Robert Wood Johnson Foundation to help young people discover something else: their ability to change the world. I spent months learning about the issues young people face in their communities. I felt their desire to fix things, and I heard their ideas on how to do so. I realized through that work the power young people have to create solutions to the world's problems. I also realized the power I have to help them. It transformed me and awakened a sense of purpose that fuels me to this day. I've since dedicated my life to feeding the good in young people and helping them to feed the good in the world. I believe that young people are not the future; they are our best hope for changing the world right now. That is why the two most important questions we can ask young people are, what are your ideas to make the world a better place, and how can I help?"

—BOBBY JONES
chief marketing and communications officer, Peace First
coauthor, *Good Is the New Cool: Market Like You Give a Damn*

"The first time I realized I could raise my voice and take an action that has impact was when I was very young. It seems almost unfathomable now, but I will never forget that I raised my voice to question my third-grade teacher about what the difference was between a thesaurus and a dictionary. My classmates and I were growing up in Midland, Texas, and I was the only Black girl. My teacher told me I

was wrong about what a thesaurus was, and she told me to come to the front of the classroom and apologize to the class. I was so young and didn't understand what was happening, but I knew it was wrong, and I was raised right. I told my teacher 'no.' I don't know why or how, but that shaped me. I knew, and still hold to the belief today, that the reason she asked me to do that was because she was intimidated and could not believe a little Black girl would push back on anyone in academia. I knew that what she was asking me to do was something I wouldn't have been asked to do had I been white or male."

—AMBER GOODWIN
founder, Community Justice Reform Coalition

"This wasn't the first time I realized I could make a difference, but it's probably the most important time. In October 2016, I went to Berlin to speak to the marketing staff of Mercedes-Benz. I had dinner the night before with two friends, and the conversation inevitably turned to the presidential election in the United States. At this point, thirty days before the election, few people believed Donald Trump would win. But the fact that Trump was one of the final two candidates astounded us.

My friends told me that they still didn't understand how their grandparents' generation could let Adolf Hitler come to power, and they saw direct parallels between Hitler and Trump. They warned me, 'If Trump wins, it will be 1930 for America.' What they meant was that before Hitler was Hitler, he was 'just' a popular politician. He didn't start exterminating Jewish people and invading countries on his first day as chancellor.

The effect of this conversation was profound. I didn't want my grandchildren to wonder if I resisted Trump, and so I started using my social media accounts to fight Trump. Few, if any, social media influencers took such an aggressive stance at the time. They didn't want to go off-topic from social media, marketing, sales, innovation, and entrepreneurship.

I wasn't going to avoid resisting Trump because I was afraid of losing followers and business. So I turned my Facebook, LinkedIn, Twitter, and Google+ into political feeds—contrary to the wisdom of so-called social media experts, who thought this would mean ruining my brand and losing followers. Quite the contrary happened. There were a few hundred people who complained about

me getting political and resisting Trump, but by far the feedback was supportive. My favorite email contained this:

*'. . . You are Guy Fuckin' Kawasaki. Who gives a shit about losing some
followers because of something you write? Your power comes from your vast
experience, by you being right, and by you being early. Don't change from those
three things.'*

*I may have lost a few hundred followers, but I gained thousands more.
Standing up for what I believed was not only the right thing to do, it also was
a good marketing decision. However, even if my stand had cost me in terms of
followers, branding, or income, I still would have done it."*

—GUY KAWASAKI
author, evangelist, technologist

*"My first foray into activism was a failure. At fifteen, I spearheaded a campaign
to get comprehensive sex education taught in my conservative hometown. After
three years of organizing, the school board roundly rejected our proposal.*

*My fight against abstinence-only programs drew the interest of documen-
tary filmmakers, and a year later* The Education of Shelby Knox *premiered on
PBS. Offers to speak about youth activism poured in but, as my efforts had
failed, I didn't know what I'd say.*

*Uncomfortable, I asked my audiences to share their experiences with
oppression and activism. In rooms from California to Maine, film screenings
turned into impromptu consciousness raising groups that touched on everything from sex ed to queer and trans' student's rights to gender and racially
motivated violence. People said they left feeling less alone, with new allies and
plans to work together to make change in their community.*

*The story of my failed campaign is how I made a difference. It encouraged
others to tell their stories, and stories build solidarity. Solidarity sparks actions,
big and small, and actions and solidarity are the cornerstones of movements.
Never underestimate the power of your story, because our stories, together, are
how we're going to win."*

—SHELBY KNOX
feminist organizer, outreach director for *Audrie & Daisy* and
Bei Bei: A Documentary

rev·o·lu·tion

/ˌrevəˈlooSH(ə)n/

"a radical and pervasive change in society and the social structure"

—Dictionary.com

"I'm scared. Can you help me?"

This is one of the jarring questions we've fielded again and again, day in and day out, from friends, family, and coworkers since Inauguration Day 2017. After the 2016 election of Donald Trump, we too were afraid of threats to our freedom (and that of our neighbors), but we wanted to move as quickly as possible from states of fear and outrage to those of action.

In rapid response to the anxiety surrounding those Election Day results, we decided to do something about it—by creating a tactical field guide to understanding, using, and defending the rights we have and to fighting for the justice that we still need to achieve. We are writers, creatives, and community builders, and we've reached out to activists, journalists, artists, public servants, and business leaders to help create and share this resource for all of you who want to make a difference in whatever way you can.

"I'm angry. How can I channel that into something positive?"

The majority of us are affected by discriminatory travel bans, attacks on reproductive freedom and sexual orientation, barriers to education and free expression, and economic anxiety about jobs, health care, and student loans. Still, this road map isn't just about being *against* a particular political policy or position. Nope. Instead, we're on a mission to demonstrate how to be *for* something, by getting more engaged in our communities, seeing and measuring progress, and protecting our rights and liberties every day (not just every four years). We believe in the power of the people, and that the adage about safety in numbers applies. A group of passionate citizens making their concerns known at a town hall meeting can move lawmakers from apathy to action quickly (if only out of self-preservation).

"I'm overwhelmed. Where do I start?"

Whatever time you have to engage is enough to make a difference. We'll show you how to be an effective advocate and make it count! You may already be an activist (or a slacktivist—no judgment here; doing anything is better than doing nothing at all!). If you can be a changemaker while saving time, you're an effective revolutionary—and you're in good company.

So, let's go!

You want to make positive change, protect your community, and take back your power (starting with your hometown), right? The sky isn't falling (yet); but if it were, wouldn't you rather be out there finding a solution instead of hiding under your bed?

We know that Rome wasn't built in a day and that tactics must be coupled with strategy and community building to form culture-shifting movements. But being proactive rather than reactive to the daily revelations of this truth-is-stranger-than-fiction world is a good position from which to start. Collaboration, consensus, and shared ideals are critical to turning ideas into action. Creating micromovements, tracking results, correcting course, and consistently building on successes that lead to tangible results are game-changing tactics. We aim to help you figure out what you want to do—and how to do it.

Is it possible to make change and still get your kid to school on time (with ten minutes to spare before the board meeting)? It is if you know where to begin. And we have your road map right here.

THE PREMISE
Think Globally, Act Locally, Scale Digitally

- Learn about the current institutions that have an impact on all of our daily lives

- Learn what it takes to bring change to those institutions

- Learn about secure tools for building your movement

- Learn winning tactics for building awareness, consciousness, and momentum

The Road Map

In the pages ahead, this simple-to-follow, boots-on-the-ground, open-anywhere guidebook delivers practical tactics for navigating, affecting, and protecting your own personal democracy in a gridlocked, heavily surveilled, and politically volatile United States. With infographics, links to resources and communities, and words of wisdom from people already fighting the good fight, this guidebook is meant to be used and abused. It's designed to move you from idea to action to part-time revolution in a quick, efficient, and effective manner.

What Will You Do?

Run for local office? Create a statewide ballot initiative? Legalize cannabis in your state? Change your company's family leave policies or your college's sexual assault policies? Institutions in this country may seem impenetrable, but in this field guide we share stories, resources, and tactics from the pros who know what to do at every level.

So let's get to it: We've got a revolution to attend to and we can't make change without you!

1

PROTESTS AND CIVIL DISOBEDIENCE

ne day after the 2017 U.S. presidential inauguration, more than 3 million people turned out worldwide to march for human rights, and explicitly gender equity. Before the Women's March on Washington (and at satellite marches around the country and globe), there was skepticism about its ability to draw large, diverse crowds. The march exceeded all expectations and projections, making it the largest demonstration in United States history and the inspiration and model for numerous marches and several ongoing move- ments that followed. The march put the world on notice that regular people from across the country were activated and ready to put feet on the street to be seen and heard. But that was only Day One. The beginning. Marches and protests are happening spontaneously and being scheduled months out, with no end in sight. Why so many? Why should you put your body and voice on the line? Because protests and civil disobedience can work wonders.

Protests and acts of civil disobedience were present at the very founding of this nation and helped create the fundamental rights protected by the Constitution. Exercising our right to free speech and freedom of assem- bly (including via protests) is as American as apple pie. Protest actions have made a huge comeback over the past few years, to a degree not seen since the late 1960s. Black Lives Matter, the Women's March, the Occupy movement, impromptu airport protests, the Standing Rock showdown over the Dakota Access Pipeline, and many more actions have brought longtime activists and regular people to the streets, to airline terminals, and to town halls, represent- ing an assembly of engaged citizens.

Protests and civil disobedience cannot be ignored or bypassed. And the frequency of citizen assembly will grow as fired-up individuals and invigorated organizations lead the way.

The internet's capabilities boost and amplify the powerful potential of such actions. As one example, much of the Arab Spring uprising of 2011 was driven online and resulted in the overthrow of a dictator in just seventeen days.

In this chapter, we will explore why protests and civil disobedience actions are go-to tools for resistance, and how you can participate with the best results.

Look ahead for explanations of the following:

- Your constitutionally guaranteed rights to speak and assemble, how they apply to your participation in protests and acts of civil disobedience, and where those rights end
- How protests and other acts of civil disobedience have led directly to tangible social, political, and policy changes
- How to boldly use social media to raise awareness, consciousness, and funds
- How to support movements and protests as an ally
- Self-care for protesters
- What to do if you're teargassed
- What to do if you're arrested

Along the way, you'll hear from a revolutionary organizer of one of the most important movements of this decade, one that changed the conversation about racism in the United States, and from a revolutionary doctor who shares her eyewitness account of using her specific skills to support the demonstrations taking place at Standing Rock on-site.

FIELD NOTES
TERMS AND CONCEPTS TO KNOW

Black Lives Matter (#BlackLivesMatter): The Movement for Black Lives, also known as Black Lives Matter (BLM), is an international, decentralized activist movement that emerged in the United States in 2013. Cofounded by Patrisse Cullors, Alicia Garza, and Opal Tometi, the movement began with the use of the social media hashtag *#BlackLivesMatter* after the acquittal of George Zimmerman in the killing of African-American teen Trayvon Martin. BLM gained global recognition for organizing protests in communities worldwide from Ferguson, Missouri, to Sweden against racial injustice, police brutality, racial profiling, economic injustice, and more.

cisgender: A person whose gender identity corresponds with the sex assigned to them at birth.

civil disobedience: An active refusal to obey policies, laws, demands, and commands of a government or of an occupying international power. Can also be applied to actions taken refusing to recognize policies of other institutional authorities, such as college administrations.

colonialism: The policy or practice of politically controlling, occupying, and exploiting another country economically and culturally. The United States was famously colonized by Great Britain, but colonization has been perpetrated on every continent. Colonialism is a social and cultural system that relies on unbalanced power relationships and unequal distribution of resources favoring the colonizers over the people who are indigenous to the occupied land.

Columbusing: This slang term describes the act of "discovering" something that is not new and is inspired by its namesake, Christopher Columbus, who ignored the fact that millions of people already inhabited the "New World" he "discovered," people he subsequently captured, displaced, and subjugated. The term emerged on the internet to serve as shorthand for forms of cultural appropriation, co-option, and erasure.

crowdfunding: Soliciting donations online from friends, colleagues, and even strangers, leveraging one of the many available digital platforms.

divestment: The opposite of investment, that is, reducing investment on moral, political, or ethical grounds. An individual, company, financial institution, pension fund, or academic institution can divest themselves of their ownership in companies or countries. The term was first used widely in the United States in the 1980s to refer to the pressure to disinvest in companies with South African origin or ties, to protest apartheid and accelerate its abolition.

#NoDAPL: The hashtag used by the Standing Rock water protectors and their supporters and allies. It means "No Dakota Access Pipeline."

nonviolent resistance: The practice of igniting social change through symbolic protests, civil disobedience, economic or political noncooperation, or other methods, without using physical force.

privilege: A person's proximity to power within social systems including white supremacy, patriarchy, heterosexism, and classism, among others, which impacts their influence and access to advantages in our culture. Look at privilege in the context of institutional power to fully understand how it functions in both our society and our lives.

transgender: People who have a gender identity or expression that differs from their assigned birth sex.

Standing Rock: The name of a Sioux reservation created as part of an 1868 treaty with the United States government. There are multiple nations represented by the term *Sioux*, including the Lakota and the Dakota nations. When the route of the Dakota Access Pipeline was changed to avoid going through Bismarck, North Dakota, and to instead impact the Standing Rock Sioux Reservation, tribal communities came together to protect the water source and sacred grounds of Standing Rock.

water protectors: Rather than call themselves "protesters," tribal communities coming together at Standing Rock chose "water protectors," representing what they stand up for rather than what they stand against.

THE CONSTITUTION AND PROTESTS

THE FIRST AMENDMENT GUARANTEES FREEDOM OF SPEECH AND THE RIGHT TO PEACEFUL ASSEMBLY

But there is a "time, place, and manner" filter. The place is public: sidewalks, streets, public plazas, parks. In other words, stay off private property (unless you have permission).

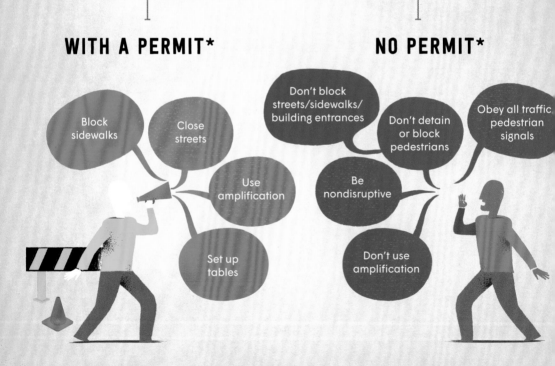

WITH A PERMIT*

- Block sidewalks
- Close streets
- Use amplification
- Set up tables

NO PERMIT*

- Don't block streets/sidewalks/building entrances
- Don't detain or block pedestrians
- Obey all traffic pedestrian signals
- Be nondisruptive
- Don't use amplification

*A fee can be charged, but there must be a waiver for those who can't afford it. You can counterdemonstrate, but police can legally separate you from your target. You'll need advance notice for a permit, unless in response to recent/current events.

HOW TO USE SOCIAL MEDIA
TO RAISE AWARENESS, CONSCIOUSNESS, AND FUNDING

Today's complex online ecosystem presents an advantage to you that organizers of yesteryear did not have. Namely: Social media allows you to distribute the messages you want to be seen far and wide. You are not bound by place, space, and time when it comes to finding people who care about your cause and spurring them to action. Raising awareness, consciousness, and even funds has never been simpler. That being said, there's a reason some people think social media = time suck. It's easy to overinvest your time and even easier to feel overwhelmed. All social media channels are not created equal for the task.

Consider this section your primer on the most appropriate tools for social media activism, as well as your permission to just say no to spending twenty-four hours a day chasing your tail on social.

RAISING AWARENESS

Know your tools for mass (but shallow) distribution (aka awareness). Some social media tools are best for disseminating quick takes. They don't necessarily drive traffic to think pieces or foster conversation; however, they are best for propagating a headline or sharing what's happening in real time. Twitter is an obvious leader in this space. Another service to look into is Thunderclap, a tool that allows you to make it easy for supporters to share coordinated messages across Facebook, Twitter, and Tumblr. You set a schedule and provide the base language for shares. Your partners connect their profiles on a one-time basis to contribute to your "Thunderclap."

Make friends with clickbait. If your goal is mass awareness and distribution, then you know what to do: Write the most pithy-yet-clicky headline you can manage. A headline that lets people get the gist of your message even if they never actually click through. And a headline that isn't so long that it discourages people from re-sharing it. The ACLU (@ACLU) has a Twitter stream full of short copy to which they add links and hashtags. Their position is very clear, and if you re-share their tweets, there is usually space for you to add commentary or to swap in your favorite hashtags.

Understand the audience mindset. People like to "spray and pray" the same content across every social media tool, but spare a thought for the mindset of your potential advocates and how it changes depending on where you reach them. Twitter has become a real-time engine—people turn to Twitter to know what's happening right now. Sometimes it's fun stuff, like #Scandal, and sometimes it's current events, like #Ferguson. So when raising awareness via tweets, try to make your updates as of-the-moment as you can, perhaps even tying other current events or trending topics to your post (avoiding irrelevant or spammy tweets, please!). Facebook, in contrast, is a place where humans come to connect with other humans, individuals they mostly consider family and friends, and skews to a slightly older demographic. Personalize as much as possible. Tell the story of why you care about this cause, this action, this issue, and so on.

A picture is worth . . . well, you know. Can your cause be captured in strong images? If so, leverage the hell out of image-oriented social media tools like Instagram, Tumblr, or Pinterest. If not, save your limited bandwidth for other tools. For example, humane societies nationwide have figured out what Sarah McLachlan always knew: Plaintive images of sad animals will stick in the brain forever. As a result, these organizations share a steady stream of such images to keep the "adopt, don't shop" message top of mind. In emergency situations, a powerful image can rally masses of people to help. For example, an image of one young Syrian refugee child who fell victim to drowning while trying to escape to Canada by way of the Greek island Kos did more to wake people up to the crisis than facts, figures, or even widely shared pictures of adult refugees did. We know that blog posts and Facebook shares get better traction when they include an image—so start thinking about what pictures bring your cause or issue to life and will make people *feel* something.

RAISING CONSCIOUSNESS

Know your tools for deeper dives. Unlike, for example, Twitter, some social media distribution channels are better designed for helping people learn more about a subject. Take, for example, Medium: It's pretty much a networked blog site containing nothing but deeper dives and think pieces.

Facebook is also a great place to engage with your network of friends and family and give them ongoing insight into your activities.

Bring your community with you via video. One of the most powerful new social media distribution mechanisms is live social video broadcasting. Facebook Live and YouTube Live (the rebranded Google Hangouts on Air) are among the biggest live video platforms on the web and conducive to videos both long and short. There are also numerous ways to share short, even ephemeral, videos via tools like Snapchat, Instagram Stories, and more. If you are feet on the street at a protest, live broadcasting brings your community with you. If you attend an important school board or city council meeting, you can provide meaningful access to those who couldn't make it to the event. Your mobile phone can create witnesses to potentially problematic interactions (without endangering yourself).

Chuck Swift's Protest Tips

Chuck Swift is the former deputy CEO of the Sea Shepherd Conservation Society and a longtime leader of protests and civil disobedience on land and sea.

Be selective. I've seen a lot of badly executed protesting. Ask questions, especially about the objectives of the action—are they clear and reasonably attainable?

The team matters. Pay attention to your group members. If someone has poor self-control, is using drugs or alcohol while planning an action, is overconfident or too interested in being in charge (or in front of cameras!)—consider those red flags, and don't be afraid to step aside if you're uncomfortable. I won't be involved in anything unless at least one person I trust has vouched for the group.

Infiltrators are real. Unless you are violating laws, which I advise against, you have nothing to worry about most of the time, but be aware. I once flew halfway across the country to help lead an action. Upon meeting with the home team to review plans, they mentioned several fishy things that had happened. After asking a series of questions, I canceled the action. I ruffled some feathers, but two members of that team eventually did real time in jail, and another was later proven to be an informer, so I regret nothing.

Know your shit. Don't be the dumbass who, when asked a question about the issues with a microphone in your face, has to admit you don't know. If you can't articulate the basic facts of the issue you are working on, find another way to participate.

Amplify marginalized voices. One of the most powerful things you can do as a part-time revolutionary is to amplify the voices of other activists, especially those representing marginalized communities. It's one thing to share your own feelings about racism, for example, but it's walking that talk even further down the path to share the words and wisdom of racial justice activists who fight that fight every single day. Find reliable sources on your favorite social media platforms, follow them, and then re-share their work directly. Use the in-platform tools for sharing so that their original share is visible to your community, and so that your community can click once and find these great voices themselves, follow them, and grow their networks. Look at your record of sharing and ask, "Am I walking my talk?"

RAISING FUNDING

Know your tools for fundraising. The current big three are Kickstarter, GoFundMe, and Indiegogo. Kickstarter, the pioneer, is most focused on makers and creators (although that can certainly include activist art or hard-hitting documentaries). GoFundMe is most commonly used for personal expenses (such as covering medical expenses, raising money for someone who was fired for standing up for what's right, and so on). Indiegogo started as a funding platform for independent film but now offers a grab bag of fundraising options. Then there are targeted tools, such as DonorsChoose for teachers fundraising for their classrooms and students, or CrowdRise and Razoo, which are standout tools for fundraising that allow you to aggre-gate fundraising of teams and to organize fundraising events and chal-lenges. A newer tool called StartSomeGood is designed for fundraising for specific social impact projects, whether you're working with a nonprofit, a community group, a social enterprise, or an individual.

Know the rules. These platforms do not all work the same. For example, Kickstarter is all or nothing: You must hit your goal to get any of the funds raised. Meanwhile, Indiegogo pays out any funds raised during the fund-raising period, whether you hit your goal or not. Check out each platform's rules regarding all-or-nothing targets, fees paid, time limits on your fund-raising period, and more. Understanding these constraints will help you not only choose a platform but also set a fundraising goal. Make sure to check the payment-processing fees each platform charges (on top of their own service fees) and check whether or not they allow donors the option to cover the processing fees for their donation. Finally, find out if the platform is rewards-based for donors. Kickstarter and Indiegogo both feature campaigns that offer some kind of reward to donors based on their level of donation. If you use one of these rewards-based platforms, make sure you can deliver what you're committing to.

Stand out in the crowd. As crowdfunding becomes more popular, it also becomes harder to grab potential funders' attention and get your project or cause shared. The upside is that with so many tools, you may be able to find one whose audience has already self-identified as being interested in your issue. The downside is that these tools are now no different than many other social media platforms. Being highlighted or featured is the best way to reach a massive audience, and it really helps to know one of the gatekeepers. Assuming you don't know a staff member at one of the crowdfunding companies, be prepared to work hard for every donated dollar. According to Kathryn Finney, founder of digitalundivided, a social enterprise that encourages entrepreneurs who are women of color and that conducted a successful campaign on Kickstarter in 2015, "The strength of your personal network is the single most important factor to a non-widget-based Kickstarter campaign." Furthermore, it takes time to build and prepare your network to activate to help you when you need them.

Build an action plan. The more effort you put in before you launch your crowdfunding campaign, the more your work to distribute and amplify that campaign will pay off. That means building your network, crafting a compelling story, and creating the words, pictures, and videos to best bring that story to life. Obviously, you can't plan emergency crowdfunding in advance, but if you do strategic crowdfunding for an ongoing cause, then expect to spend as much time preparing to launch a campaign as you will during the campaign itself. It's an investment to seek investment, so plan your time accordingly. The bonus is that you not only raise money, you also build a community of people who care about your cause—so it's time well spent.

⬡ TOOLS FOR THE TASK | LIVE BROADCASTING

Tool	Live, Limited Time, or Live+Recorded	What You Should Know
Facebook Live	Live+Recorded	You can share publicly, with friends only, or even to specific Facebook groups. Viewers can comment.
Instagram Video	Live	Access to view is same as at account level: If you're a private feed, only your followers can see it; however, if you're a public feed, everyone can see it.
Snapchat Live Stories	Limited Time	As a Snapchat user, you have a "Story," and you can add Snaps to it anytime, but each individual Snap stays in the Story for only 24 hours. It can be a great way to share your everyday activism.
YouNow	Live	You can raise funds via a cut of the real money viewers use to buy virtual gifts.
YouTube Live	Live+Recorded	You must have at least 100 subscribers to be able to do YouTube Live streaming from your mobile device. Google Hangouts on Air is now part of YouTube Live.

⬢ TOOLS FOR THE TASK | CROWDFUNDING

Tool	All or Nothing?	Fees	What You Should Know
CrowdRise	No	Range of pricing plans: fundraising .crowdrise.com /nonprofit-pricing	Designed for people to raise money for charities. Donors and fundraisers get "impact points." You can have an individual page or create an event page to track a team of fundraisers, including by publishing a leaderboard.
GoFundMe	No	5%, plus payment processing fees	Not community-based; all funding will come through your network and sharing.
Indiegogo	Optional	5%, plus payment processing fees	They encourage a campaign duration of 40 days or fewer. Rewards-based.
KickStarter	Yes	5%, plus payment processing fees	Focused on creative projects, such as film, art, and technology. Rewards-based.
Rally	No	5%, plus payment processing fees	Cause-oriented, but official nonprofit status is not required.
Razoo	No	4% or 5%, depending on whether a charity or not, plus payment processing fees	Similar to CrowdRise in that it lets you form fundraising teams, but also lets you fundraise for anything.
StartSomeGood	Yes	5% (if project is funded), plus payment processing fees	Focused on projects with specific goals for social impact, and each project will be vetted before it is allowed to be launched on the site.

WHY MARCHES AND

The moves we make can impact the next waves of everyday revolution-aries. Here's how grassroots tactics fought, won, and reclaimed lost ground with continued commitment from each generation.

ANTI-LYNCHING MOVEMENT

THE 1890s
Ida B. Wells condemned lynching in the pamphlet *Southern Horrors: Lynch Law in All Its Phases*.

1916
The National Association for the Advancement of Colored People (NAACP) raises awareness about lynching. The anti-lynching play *Rachel* by Angelina Weld Grimké debuts.

1937
Juanita Jackson Mitchell per-suades NBC to broadcast about anti-lynching laws.

1930S-1960s
NAACP youth groups mobilize with meetings, selling buttons, poster campaigns, and demonstrations in 80 cities.

MONTGOMERY BUS BOYCOTT: A SNAPSHOT

1954
Professor Jo Ann Robinson met with the city of Montgomery about ending segregation on city transit.

1955

March Claudette Colvin is arrested for refusing to give up her seat on the bus to a white passenger.

October Mary Louise Smith is arrested for not giving up her seat, becoming a plaintiff in a lawsuit.

December Public buses are desegregated in Montgomery.

November Supreme Court of the United States upholds the ruling deeming segrega-tion on buses illegal.

June A federal district court rules that segregated buses are unconstitutional.

FROM #JUSTICE4TRAYVON

2012

February In an act of vigilante violence, George Zimmerman kills Trayvon Martin in Sanford, Florida.

March The Million Hoodies Movement for Justice holds rallies calling for Zimmerman's arrest. A Change.org petition garners more than 1.3 million signatures. Representative Bobby Rush is removed from the House floor for wear-ing a hoodie in solidarity.

#BlackLivesMatter protests emerge from Missouri to New York in response to the deaths of Michael Brown and Eric Garner at the hands of police.

2014

July 20 Enormous crowds show up for protests calling for justice for Trayvon Martin; 1,000 dem-onstrators stage a sit-in in Times Square in New York City.

PROTESTS MATTER

1917
10,000 African Americans march in the Silent Parade protest in New York City.

1918
The Dyer Anti-Lynching Bill is introduced.

1919
Demonstrations organized in response to race riots during the Red Summer.

1935
Senators introduce the Costigan-Wagner Bill "to assure to persons . . . equal protection of the crime of lynching." Dixiecrats hinder progress.

1920s
16 Black women formed the Anti-Lynching Crusaders to fundraise to pass the Dyer Bill, engaging in organized prayer and direct-action campaigns. Dixiecrats filibuster (using prolonged speech to obstruct a legislative measure) the bill.

December 1–2 NAACP member Rosa Parks ignites a movement. Women's Political Council launches a bus boycott.

December 8–13 The Montgomery Improvement Association organizes a carpool for Black boycott participants.

March Martin Luther King Jr. is indicted and forced to pay $500. He is incarcerated for 386 days.

February 80 boycott leaders are indicted due to anti-conspiracy laws in Alabama.

1956

TO THE BIRTH OF #BLACKLIVESMATTER

April The Congressional Black Caucus introduces H.Res.612 in honor of Trayvon Martin. The Dream Defenders start a 40-mile protest. George Zimmerman is charged with second-degree murder.

June Sanford police chief Bill Lee is fired.

July 14 Patrisse Cullors tags a social media post about Zimmerman's acquittal with the hashtag *#BlackLivesMatter*. Alicia Garza, Patrisse Cullors, and Opal Tometi found Black Lives Matter.

July 13 George Zimmerman is acquitted.

2013

PATRISSE CULLORS

COFOUNDER, BLACK LIVES MATTER

In 2013, George Zimmerman was acquitted in the killing of teenager Trayvon Martin, and the hashtag *#BlackLivesMatter* was born. The hashtag birthed a movement and an organization, cofounded by three queer Black women activists: Alicia Garza, Opal Tometi, and Patrisse Cullors. Black Lives Matter is now an international organization with chapters across North America. According to their site, blacklivesmatter.com, "#BlackLivesMatter is working for a world where Black lives are no longer systematically and intentionally targeted for demise."

Patrisse is an artist and lifelong community organizer. When Black Lives Matter was born, she ran the Los Angeles–based Dignity and Power Now, a grassroots organization focused on helping prisoners in L.A. County, and pushed for sheriff accountability. Much of her work before cofounding Black Lives Matter was also focused locally.

From Hashtag to Movement

"In the wake of Zimmerman's acquittal, Alicia spoke out to Black people on Twitter, saying 'our lives matter,' and I put a hashtag in front of it, and Opal chimed in with a vision for an organization around the concept. Things happened pretty quickly. Within days we were talking about what it would look like to give Black folks across the globe a way to talk about racism in their own settings. It was an online social media campaign, but it was also something we wanted to see taken to the streets. When we saw people holding signs saying '#BlackLivesMatter,' standing in front of the tanks in Ferguson, Missouri, after Michael Brown was killed, we said, 'Whoa, we created something.'

"We decided to organize a six-hundred-person Black Lives Matter ride into Ferguson, which I led. It was our first time leading such an action as an organization. We decided during that action that, going forward, there would be two lanes of responsibility. First, we would stay in solidarity with the people of Ferguson—we spent the next year working on the ground there supporting them. But second, we needed to go home and do the work to develop local chapters, because Ferguson is not an aberration."

Patrisse is the author of the new book *When They Call You a Terrorist—A Black Lives Matter Memoir*, released in January 2018.

"Be part of a local movement with national implications."

Managing Decentralized Growth under Guiding Principles

"We didn't originally call ourselves 'founders,' but we started to see ourselves being erased from the narrative about Black Lives Matter, particularly as queer Black women. We also saw the political ideals integral to the movement being stripped from it. Things like being explicitly anti-white supremacy and patriarchy, pro-queer and trans rights, and so on. So we intervened.

"We felt it was important to be decentralized, but created a set of guiding principles, to help shape the agenda and give a framework for the way in which we work for Black people. We identify places and spaces that are harmful to Black people, and the work needed to address them—and gain the power to reclaim monies, land, and resources.

"We're grateful for the chapters across the world that have aligned themselves with the principles of Black Lives Matter. They represent a generation of disruptors, doing the work.

"The network connects via digital channels and phone calls. It's rare we meet in person, and yes, we are really worried about the security of our communications. We know that we're being surveilled, so we're working on using more secure platforms."

"Collective Care" > Self-Care

"We message to our community before marches or protests: what to do, who to call if there's trouble. We try to prepare for danger, because any time there's law enforcement present, anything can happen. We want to share information about how to take care of yourself . . . but also how to take care of each other.

"We try to make an example of how we need to be taking care of ourselves, not just as individuals, but as a collective. I call it 'collective care.'

"As someone who was an artist before I was politicized, this includes art and cultural work, which are important cornerstones for me, and have always been the backbone of Black movements."

Black Lives Matter in the Trump Era

"Since the 2016 election, white folks have shifted their focus to Trump. And the national media only wants to cover Trump. But Black people haven't forgotten about Black people. And our work was never just to have national visibility. The local is national.

"It's unfortunate the news media isn't calling on Black people to talk about the issues in our government, since so many of them affect Black people. Don't think the work isn't happening because it's not getting the same national media attention.

"If you want to help: Join something. I'm not a big fan of individuals doing something out there, flailing a little, when they can be part of a local movement with national implications. The second thing you can do: Have the hard conversations. With your family. Friends. Talk about Black Lives Matter. About the killing of Black trans women. About the high depression rates. About issues in the Black community. Organize monies to move something forward. Donate toward a Black organization."

ALLY-SUPPORTED MOVEMENTS

From the civil rights movement to the Women's March, many of the most impactful social and political movements emerge from historically oppressed communities organizing themselves to combat systemic injustices. If showing up for a community that is not your own intimidates you, know that you are not alone and that you can make a difference if you know how to engage.

If the goal is to commit yourself to justice, open yourself up to learning and don't be afraid to make mistakes. The result will be uniting with others by being your best self—even if it's a work in progress.

Here is a checklist of the seven habits of highly effective allies.

1. OWN YOUR PRIVILEGE

Recognize your rewards. People are often given unearned advantages or benefits because of identities that are imbued with a higher value by society or normalized in the dominant culture. In the United States, such privilege is most often associated with whiteness, cisgender maleness, heterosexuality, physical and mental ability, documented citizenship, and material wealth.

Study systems of power and how you fit into them. There are long histories of homophobia, transphobia, racism, colonialism, sizeism, sexism, ageism, ableism, Islamophobia, anti-Semitism, economic injustice, and other injustices in our society. If you do not belong to one of these frequently targeted groups, you have the privilege of not experiencing such covert and overt aggressions.

Resist defensiveness and embrace compassion. Acknowledge that being born with privilege may have sheltered you from certain realities about discrimination and suffering. Transform your feelings of guilt into hard work to counter those injustices.

Adapted from the previously published "Allied Force: A guide to showing up without getting in the way" by Jamia Wilson, *Rookie*, 01/14/15.

2. BE VULNERABLE, APPROPRIATELY

Expect to be uncomfortable. Be willing to learn, even if it means that you could be called out for not knowing something. If your words or actions are challenged, and it makes you feel embarrassed or humiliated, consider it education or a rite of passage.

Humans make mistakes. Don't let a misstep keep you from supporting causes you care about. After such an experience, journal about what you have learned and seek to do differently, and make a pledge to be a better listener and more thoughtful communicator.

Know Your Biases

You may be familiar with the terms (and damaging effects of) *racism* and *sexism*, but these are not the only biases that individuals and societies can perpetuate. Individual biases are all too often reinforced by policy, laws, media messages, corporate interests, and even our educational systems. Check out this list of other biases that, like racism and sexism, can take the form of disgust, fear, hatred, and violence along with other forms of systemic discrimination.

ableism: A range of discriminatory attitudes and practices that devalue people with disabilities in favor of nondisabled people. Ableist policies and institutions are those that limit people with disabilities' access to power, services, and support.

ageism: Discrimination, bias, stereotyping, or prejudice on the basis of a person's age. Like other forms of discrimination, ageism can be implicit or explicit. *Adultism* is the term for a bias toward adults that undermines younger people, while *jeunism* is the term for bias that discriminates against older people in favor of youth.

homophobia: A range of negative attitudes, stereotypes, prejudices, and irrational fears of lesbian, gay, bisexual, and transgender people.

sizeism: Discrimination based on a person's physical size, including both weight and height.

transphobia: A range of negative attitudes, stereotypes, prejudices, and irrational fears specifically of transgender and other gender-nonconforming people.

Take responsibility. Prepare to apologize as necessary, and when you do, be sincere and don't make it about you; don't be defensive, and never work from the dreaded "I'm sorry you felt that way" non-apology playbook.

Get support and seek connection. If you have feelings of helplessness, confusion, or shame and reactions like outrage, fear, or sadness, ask for support from a therapist or other allies. Working out (or on) your guilt or anger with people who are dealing with oppression can hurt more than it helps.

3. LISTEN MORE THAN YOU TALK

Listen and learn. When a person expresses frustration about oppression that you haven't personally experienced, it's a good time to listen. Even if your intentions are good, diminishing people's stories does more to advance oppression than dismantle it.

Show up, don't show off. When publicly supporting a movement, spend time sharing the voices of that movement and the communities it supports. For example, you can find, follow, and regularly retweet the Twitter feeds of activists leading the work on the ground. Highlight their work and insights more than promoting your own.

4. FACE YOUR FEARS

Shake hands with your fear. If you believe in something but are reluctant to speak out about it, ask yourself what you're afraid of.

Investigate your concerns. Are you afraid of hostility from family members and friends with different beliefs? Are you worried that you're not well enough informed to take a firm stand? What are the concrete consequences if those fears come true?

Consider the cost of your silence. Are these potential consequences you're imagining more important than being true to your values? Weigh the consequences of staying silent, then think about what steps you can take to feel supported by like-minded people if you speak out and do face backlash.

5. DON'T TRY TO "SAVE" ANYONE

Save yourself. There is a quote by Australian Indigenous activist Lilla Watson that has been used as a human rights motto around the world: "If you have come here to help me, you are wasting your time. But if you have come because your liberation is bound up with mine, then let us work together." In other words, being an ally is not about being a savior—it's about understanding that your own freedom is inextricable from the freedom of oppressed communities.

6. SHOW UP

SOCIAL MEDIA TIP
How You Share on Social Media Matters

You've found some fantastic resources from within movements, and you want to amplify their voices. Be mindful that how you share their voices online matters. It is preferable to retweet an original source tweet rather than sharing someone's share of a share of a share or taking someone's wise words and tweeting them yourself (even if you give the original poster credit in your tweet). This kind of direct amplifying of activist voices allows more people to discover your sources for themselves, instead of placing you as the gatekeeper between those sources and your followers.

Be present and be active. This is an essential part of being a true ally. It means different things, depending on the cause, but if you're offering support in a way that is meaningful and sensitive to the needs of the people directly affected, you're showing up. Sometimes this involves volunteering, marching, signing petitions, sending supplies, documenting actions, offering rides, sending texts or making phone calls, or making donations. Work with your gifts. If you're a designer, design. If you're a writer, write. There are many ways to show up and be an ally. The key is to do it when, where, and how you're really needed and most potent—not just when it's convenient.

7. RESPECT MOVEMENT BUILDERS

Don't reinvent the wheel. Don't assume you know best, or are the first to think of a solution. Research tactics already in use and ask questions about the most helpful ways to support.

Do your homework. The more informed you are about a movement's history, the more effective you'll be as an ally. Educate yourself with the movement's key articles, books, speeches, and films. Seek out diverse and inclusive media sources to get up to date on current perspectives. Find and follow thought leaders on social media platforms.

Give credit where it's due. Cite sources and note their contributions to the movement. Avoid cultural appropriation or Columbusing anyone's work—or a movement itself.

Pass the mic. If you're asked to speak on behalf of a movement, pass the mic to people who are directly affected. You will help their voices be heard. It's a form of erasure to cut out the originators of ideas, and it's especially harmful when it happens to people from already marginalized communities.

The moral of the story: Always attribute words or ideas to the person or movement who created them (and if it's online, link to or tag them).

BONUS: PUT YOUR MONEY WHERE YOUR MOUTH IS

Vote with your wallet. Gloria Steinem says, "We can tell our values by looking at our checkbook stubs." If you can financially contribute to support movements outside of your own identity group or community, then do so. If you don't have access to cash, contribute transportation, online support, skills, translation expertise, access to other potential donors in your network, or other resources. Most organizations will happily tell you what they need.

DR. TARA SOOD

EMERGENCY PHYSICIAN WITH A FOCUS ON KEEPING ACTIVISTS ACTIVATING IN THE FIELD

In mid-2016, Dr. Tara Sood took a one-year sabbatical, intending to volunteer with Doctors Without Borders. When Dr. Sood fell ill right around the date of her planned departure, the organization told her to hold off, and instead she spent her sabbatical traveling from Standing Rock to Syrian refugee squats to Tanzania on a revolutionary journey to use her skills for good.

From Doctor to Activist

"In mid-2016, when my Doctors Without Borders deployment fell through, I was left with planned downtime but no mission. I started volunteering for the Hillary Clinton presidential campaign, and November brought two inflection points for me:

- The outcome of the election.
- More attention directed to the water protectors' protest of the Dakota Access Pipeline being routed through Standing Rock, and law enforcement responding with violence.

"My concern was more than caring about the environmental and cultural impact of the proposed Dakota Access Pipeline; it was knowing that what our government was doing was wrong:

- Rerouting the pipeline through Standing Rock because the city of Bismarck complained about the impact.
- Allowing the oil industry to hire security companies and to use the police against the people they should be protecting.

"What did I know? I knew they were camped out there, and that it was cold. A friend of mine introduced me to a doctor who was involved in medical care in camp. I didn't arrange through organizers. I just spoke to this doctor on the phone once and showed up. No arrangements, no plan."

Elders, Doers, and "Protest Tourists"

"I had no idea what it was going to be like. I'd never even been camping. I didn't know about wearing a 'base layer.' I had no gear. I had zero idea what I was doing or how to prepare.

Dr. Tara Sood is continuing her medical activism. From Standing Rock, she traveled to Greece to help Syrian refugees squatting in abandoned buildings, then to Tanzania to help a local physician set up and properly provision an intensive care unit (ICU) in their hospital, and then back again to Greece to continue her contributions there.

The Most Common Medical Ailments in Camp

- Coughs (exacerbated by the wood-burning stoves and the burning of sage)
- Common colds
- Outbreaks of diarrhea
- Hypothermia . . . and that brings us to what the authorities were doing to the water protectors (see "Police Brutality," opposite).

"I showed up in Cannon Ball, North Dakota (the largest community near the Standing Rock protests), at a basketball gym that was acting as an evacuation center for people too old or sick to remain in camp. Two nurses, retired friends from Portland, were there, as was an ob-gyn who had been volunteering for a few days and was just leaving. They showed me around the gym, where there was no heat, but it was indoors. People were sleeping on cots and bleachers. Supplies were stored. There was a kitchen, bathrooms, and showers. We also had a place to sit and talk to people to see what their needs were. If they needed to go to the hospital in Bismarck, no ambulance would come if called, so someone had to volunteer to drive them. Someone always did.

"There was every type of person there. There were people who felt left out in their own worlds and found community. There were 'protest tourists': kids who sought to socially document their 'commitment,' when in reality, they sat around and did nothing. But mostly there were regular, everyday people who felt they had to do something to fight against the injustice. Nurses, lawyers, veterans, Marines, students, homemakers, farmers, journalists, construction workers, engineers—people from every walk of life. The majority of the people felt they were fighting for a cause bigger than themselves. I'd say the ratio of committed individuals to protest tourists was probably 500:1. Most of the people in camp helped in every way they could—including cleaning the compost toilets, shoveling massive amounts of snow, cooking, cleaning, building shelters, hooking up solar panels, and more.

"There was little formal organization. However, if you were a native elder, people deferred to you. There was a sense of respect. Every female elder was called 'Grandmother.'

"Of the one hundred to two hundred people who were in that gym on any given day, only a handful of folks stayed at the gym; the vast majority were in camp, and they preferred to be in camp.

"Ultimately the gym–cum–evacuation center was shut down because the city needed to take back the space to use for upcoming planned Christmas activities. So after one week, I headed out to the Oceti Sakowin Camp, the encampment that was closest to direct protest actions."

Scene at Standing Rock

"At the Oceti camp, there was a medic/
healer council and section. There was an
herbalist, midwives, mental health practi-
tioners, EMTs, paramedics, social workers, body workers, nurses, and another
new doctor.

"It was not truly organized, and there
was no medical supply chain. We didn't
always have resources needed to take care
of people. You'd hope to catch people going
into Bismarck and give them a list of things
that were needed. People were taking back
roads because the police had closed the
highway. Those of us at Standing Rock had
to take alternate routes to get to Bismarck.

"Large numbers of donations were coming in, but because of the lack of organization, the donations often weren't providing
what was really needed. As an example,
when news got out that the authorities were
teargassing the water protectors, people
started sending Mylanta, but we had bottles and bottles long after it wasn't needed
anymore. Or people sent heat packs that
can't be stored below certain temperatures
and so were useless. We had a few supplies, but not necessarily the right amounts
of the right things.

"I saw people who willingly sacrificed
treatments or medications they needed
because there was such limited supply,
in case 'someone else needed it more.'
This also seemed so different from the
real world."

Police Brutality

"The typical story was that the police would
arrest people, strip them, and put them in
buses with no heat, hence the hypothermia. There were reportedly beatings, and I
saw lacerations and one woman who lost
an eye to a rubber bullet. Many Americans
can't imagine the level of mistreatment
that happened at Standing Rock—right
here in the U.S. We were witness to the
courage of the protestors at Standing
Rock as well as to the brutality of those
sent to 'protect us.' Three weeks at camp
changed my life and informed my future
activist activities.

"The camp was one of the most soulfully
powerful places I've ever been. I brought
nothing to eat or drink, and every day people would bring me supplies and check on
my well-being. There was such a strong
sense of community.

"Coming back was harder than I expected.
In addition to witnessing difficult 'this can't
be happening' experiences, I returned to
hear from people in my life who seemed
curious about my work there, but who didn't
really care about what was happening. But
Standing Rock inspires me to continue."

What Next?

"Only two months after President Trump's
inauguration, and with his urging, the
Dakota Access Pipeline project was
resumed, completed, and is nearly
ready to go.

"What can we do? Fight for divestment from the fossil fuel industry as we once fought for divestment from apartheid South Africa. So think about all the organizations you can encourage to divest:

- Individual municipalities can divest; check out the investments your city is holding, for example via pension funds, and encourage your city officials to divest.
- Large academic endowments can divest too, so look into the investments your alma mater has made, and make your voice heard as an alumnus who doesn't want university money in the fossil fuel industry.
- Check out your investments in stocks and mutual funds, including via your 401(K). If you're a direct shareholder in fossil fuel companies, sell it. If you're invested in funds that are invested, divest from those funds.
- You can learn more about the ongoing struggle at www.defunddapl.org."

Want to Be a Revolutionary Healer like Tara?

Here are some resources where medical professionals can bring skills and healing powers to activists around the globe:

www.cureblindness.com

www.doctorsoftheworld.org

www.doctorswithoutborders.org

www.operationsmile.org

www.rescue.org

www.sams-usa.net

www.whitehelmets.org

And you can find many, many more listings here: www.imva.org/pages/orgdb/wblstfrm.htm

SELF-CARE FOR PROTESTORS

Whether you're going on a one-day protest march or participating in a long-term occupation, you can't stick it out and do your best if you don't take care of yourself. Dr. Tara Sood offers this handy list of self-care to-dos to help protesters stay healthy in adverse conditions.

BEFORE YOU GO

Field audit: Don't be in the field if you have unresolved or untreated physical or mental health issues—all problems will be magnified. Dr. Sood says, "Take care of your own shit before you show up."

Field Supplies

- Hand sanitizer and wet wipes
- Nutritious, portable food you know you can rely on
- Pain relievers, Band-Aids, anti-nausea and prescribed medication
- The right gear for the environmental factors (from comfortable shoes to extreme weather gear)
- Water filtration tools or tablets
- Something that makes you happy: a lotion you like, a great book, a beloved picture, and so on

WHILE YOU'RE THERE

Physically: Wash your hands. Don't forget to eat and drink clean food and water. Don't over-imbibe! It's a protest, not a party. If your clothes get wet, and you have even just a blanket to change into, take off your clothes ASAP. Being cold and wet is worse than just being cold, and can accelerate hypothermia. Mentally: Don't get sucked into rumors, conspiracies, or unfounded gossip.

REENTRY

Coming home can be painful. You can feel proud of your experience participating while still wishing you didn't have to be out there to begin with. You may feel disconnected from it all. Upon return, you'll be different. These are common reactions—you don't have to figure it all out right away. Acknowledge and respect your conflicting feelings. Give yourself time to adjust to the "real world."

WHAT TO DO IF TEARGASSED

If you're attending a protest, march, or occupation, there may be a police presence and potential exposure to tear gas. Tear gas reacts with water, so your immediate instincts may be the opposite of what you need to do. Even if the possibility of tear gas exposure seems remote, here's a guide on how to prepare for it and act quickly if it occurs:

BEFORE YOU GO

- Tear gas crystals are activated by water, but tear gas is also absorbed (therefore prolonging its symptoms) by oil-based creams, sunscreens, and makeup. Avoid wearing those.
- The only thing that protects you 100 percent from tear gas is a real gas mask with a filter. These can cost more than $100.
- An escape hood (often marketed for use in house fires) is a second, cheaper option but is not as effective. A builder's mask is a similar choice. A dust or surgical mask is better than nothing.
- Swim goggles are a good option to protect your eyes.
- The DIY approach: Bring a rag, scarf, or bandanna that you keep tucked away. Because tear gas crystals are reactivated by exposure to water and other liquids, do not soak these rags!

WHILE EXPOSED TO TEAR GAS

- Only a gas mask truly protects you, but if your only option is some kind of cloth or holding your jacket or shirt over your mouth and nose, use the inside, which won't have been as exposed to the tear gas.
- Bring and use swim goggles.
- Do not rub your eyes or skin, as you may intensify the effects.

- Get high. Tear gas is heavier than air, so it sinks toward the ground. Stand and climb to higher ground.
- As you move, spread your arms out wide and let the air and wind remove particles from your clothes.

AFTER TEAR GAS EXPOSURE

- If you cannot shower and change clothes immediately, attempt to wash your hands thoroughly with soap and hot water.
- Take out contacts or clean glasses with soapy water after you wash your hands. Wash exposed hands before attempting to rinse out eyes by pouring water in them from your hands.
- Until you reach a safe place to shower and change, stay dry, because water effects the tear gas crystals.
- Either discard or wash your clothing multiple times. Washing in hot water and detergent is preferable to discarding what is essentially hazardous material in the trash.
- Don't take a bath, as you will be "soaking in it"; shower using lots of soap and water.
- Tear gas is most dangerous for those with respiratory ailments. If your respiratory symptoms don't subside in about an hour, seek medical assistance.

GETTING ARRESTED
HOW TO DEAL WITH LAW ENFORCEMENT, POLICE, IMMIGRATION AGENTS, OR FBI ENCOUNTERS

Let's face it: Getting arrested feels crummy, and you have way better things to do than be stuck in jail. But if you end up detained or in police custody, it helps to know your rights and to be prepared. Whether you're picked up at a protest in a mass arrest, or a routine traffic stop escalates, here are some tips for protecting yourself and your civil liberties:

BEFORE YOU GO TO A PROTEST OR DEMONSTRATION

Do your homework and know your risks. Determine whether or not the rally organizers have a permit, and research what counts as violations in your area. For example, many states have anti-masking laws that prevent people from concealing their faces, which can include bandannas. Some protesters in the Occupy movement were targeted with anti-masking laws. As we outline in the "Learn Your Rights" infographic on page 10, members of law enforcement are empowered to hold individuals and groups account-able to "time, place, and manner" restrictions without technically violating your First Amendment rights. Review the potentially prohibited actions in the graphic (such as blocking pedestrians, building entrances, traffic, or intersections without a permit; congregating on private property without permission; or using sound amplifiers that violate noise ordinances without a permit). Any one of these can be used to justify police intervention.

Know your status. Terms and conditions for arrest, search, and seizure are not guaranteed to be the same for people without U.S. citizenship. If you're undocumented or living in the United States on a green card or a visa, different rules apply, and those rules have been volatile. Before attending demonstrations or rallies, contact an immigration lawyer or your local branch of the American Civil Liberties Union to research the latest information on your rights and determine how your immigration status impacts your options and your level of risk.

Lawyer up and note your trusted contacts on your hands and arms. You have the right to representation. Before attending a demonstration, write the number of your private lawyer (if you have one) and the number for the National Lawyers Guild on your hand with a permanent marker, and program it into your phone. If the event you're attending has a legal contact, note that number as well. You might be wondering, "Why write on myself?" It is important to record key contact information and a calling-card number on your arm in case your device and other belongings are seized. It also shows that you're prepared and mean business if you're detained.

Carry the card. Download, read, and print out the ACLU's wallet card and keep it on you. It tells you what to do if you are detained by the police, immigration agents, or the FBI. Visit shop.aclu.org to get a Know Your Rights card. If you are deaf or hard of hearing, visit aclu.org/deafrights for an American Sign Language (ASL) video about deaf rights and how to deal with police encounters.

Wear layers and comfortable shoes. Dress for the possibility that you might end up in a holding cell or a blockade at a demonstration. Wear clothing that can protect you from a wide range of weather changes.

Pack light. Leave personal property at home, except for ID, meds, and quarters for the precinct phone. If you know you'll be arrested due to an act of civil disobedience, or you think it is highly likely, take two forms of ID with you—with picture ID being the best option.

If you have a medical condition, pack your medication in its pharmacy-issued prescription bottle or inhaler package. These precautions can help your arresting officer complete a Medical Treatment of Prisoner form recording the details on your prescription bottle, including the exact medication type (generic or brand), dosing information, and the name and telephone number for your prescribing pharmacy and doctor.

Keep the change. Bring quarters for telephone calls.

Consider your crew. If you were protesting with other people, think about how your words and actions might affect them in the event of an arrest. Talk about whether or not they might get fired or deported. Make sure you have conversations up front about what commitments and situations you are comfortable with and get your script together.

IF YOU'RE APPROACHED BY LAW ENFORCEMENT

Remain silent and ask for a lawyer. Take cops seriously when they say, "Anything you say can and will be used against you." Respond by articulating and exercising your constitutional rights. If you are a citizen, you can politely state that you are peacefully protesting and that your rights to peaceful assembly and free speech are protected under the First

Amendment. In some states, you may be required to share your name as a way of identifying yourself. If they continue to hold you and begin asking you additional questions, say, "Officer, I will remain silent. I'd like to speak with a lawyer." You are not legally bound to answer queries without a lawyer. Keep your hands where the officer can see them. #RealTalk: If you are from a community that has been historically targeted by state violence, be especially mindful that if you feel like your civil rights have been undermined, and you're considering expressing it to your arresting officers, know you can file an official complaint later, and although it should never have to be this way, it may be safer to do so.

Just say "no" to searches. Law enforcement may not need a warrant to search or confiscate illegal items that they can see out in the open. Don't offer up personal items that aren't in plain sight. You aren't obliged to consent to searches or seizures. State your case clearly and calmly: "Officer, I do not consent to searches of my private property." You have the right to remain silent and to refuse to consent to a search, but it could impact you later in court.

Assert your rights, but don't escalate. Don't use physical force. If officers start behaving aggressively, you can consider asking protest observers with smartphones to record the arrest on camera. You can also state clearly and audibly that you are not resisting arrest and you do not consent to any searches. Ask for their card and badge number so that people who are recording can capture this information. If you don't feel comfortable with this option, you can choose to remain silent until you speak with an attorney.

Follow physical directives and don't physically resist. Avoid doing anything that can be misconstrued as you resisting arrest. If they say, "Lie down," do it. Do not run. It will escalate the situation.

Find out if you can leave, and if you can, move on. If you have been detained at a protest and you're unsure whether you can leave, ask, "Am I free to go?" If the officer gives you an answer that is unclear, ask them again, "Am I being detained, or am I free to go?" If the answer is that you may or will be arrested, remain silent and ask to speak to a lawyer.

IF YOU'RE DETAINED OR LOCKED UP

Choose your words wisely. Be respectful and cooperative and speak in a measured tone. Refrain from name-calling or using profanity, which almost always won't help your situation, even if the authorities are acting rude and inappropriately themselves.

Call your attorney immediately, or telephone a family member or friend who can reach out for help. Remember that your calls are being recorded and be mindful about what you disclose.

Stand up for yourself. Don't forget that officers are expected to obey the law, just like you. If you believe your rights have been violated while in custody, contact your lawyer or ask for a public defender. You can also issue a complaint to a civil monitoring organization and/or the police department itself if you feel it is safe to do so.

Beware of caller ID. Don't call your office or anyone else you don't want to disclose your status to from the jail phone. Ask a lawyer or friend to connect you via a three-way call so the number that shows up on your boss's caller ID doesn't reveal that you're at central booking.

Mind your business. Don't feel pressured to talk or, worse, to get involved in a brawl. Do whatever you can to avoid extending your jail time. Keep information close and relay it on a need-to-know basis.

Even if you follow these guidelines, we can't guarantee that law enforcement will always follow the rules or won't use excessive force. If you feel that your rights have been violated in any context with law enforcement, contact the ACLU.

> The National Lawyers Guild Mass Defense Committee provides resources, legal training, and support for activists and social justice movements.
> Visit https://www.nlg.org /massdefensecommittee for more information and legal support hotlines.

TAKEAWAYS AND RESOURCES

Taking to the streets has become a mainstream pursuit these days, so remember these lessons:

Self-Care Matters

All the clichés are true. You need to put on your own oxygen mask before you can help others. It's a marathon, not a sprint. If you're a part-time revolutionary, we want you in it for the long haul. So take care of *you*—but heed the wise words of Patrisse Cullors and place high value on the concept of "collective care" too.

Be Prepared

Whatever action you're taking, long- or short-term, risky or cakewalk, think like a Scout and be prepared. Know what you're getting into, and bring supplies, snacks, and water!

Minimize Your Digital Fingerprints

Before you participate in protests, especially an act of civil disobedience, secure your data, log off unnecessary social channels and devices, and think before you post. Anything you say, do, and post can be held against you!

Better Safe than Sorry

You probably won't get teargassed or arrested. But knowing the tips in this chapter will sure come in handy in the unlikely event you have those experiences.

Your Skills Matter

Lawyers rushed to airports and lent a hand when the Trump administration first attempted to implement a Muslim ban. Mental health professionals and massage therapists volunteered at Standing Rock. Movements need accountants, marketers, writers, drivers, translators, and so much more. Pitch in!

RESOURCE LINKS

Standing Rock Reservation websites
https://www.standingrock.org and
standwithstandingrock.net

Black Lives Matter website
https://blacklivesmatter.com

**The guiding principles of
Black Lives Matter**
https://blacklivesmatter.com/about/
what-we-believe

**Kathryn Finney on "How to Win at
Kickstarter"**
https://medium.com/thelist/
how-to-win-at-kickstarter-e4f3277eba62

**The ACLU's guide to your rights at
protests and demonstrations**
https://aclu.org/sites/default/files/
field_pdf_file/kyr_protests.pdf

**The CDC's web page on riot control
preparedness**
https://emergency.cdc.gov/agent/
riotcontrol/factsheet.asp

**Kimberlé Crenshaw on
intersectionality**
https://racialequitytools.org/
resourcefiles/mapping-margins.pdf

Peggy McIntosh on privilege
https://nationalseedproject.org/
white-privilege-unpacking-the-
invisible-knapsack

John Scalzi on privilege
https://whatever.scalzi.com/2012/
05/15/straight-white-male-the-lowest-
difficulty-setting-there-is

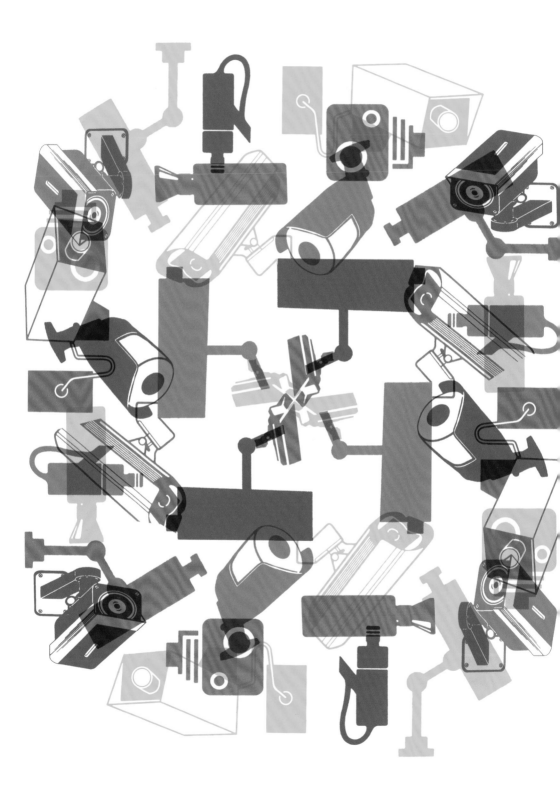

2

PROTECTING YOURSELF ONLINE AND OFF

he state of the Union: mass surveillance, the privatization of the internet, device search and confiscation at U.S. borders—these represent just some of the opportunities for our privacy and personal digital footprints to be compromised every day.

Particularly after 9/11, our brave new world includes surveillance cameras everywhere: in banks, office buildings, and public areas. According to a 2016 Google consumer survey, an average working American is caught on camera fifty to seventy-five times per day.

Additionally, we depend on the internet and social media. It's not just important for us to function day to day; it's also the connective tissue that binds communities together, including activist communities. The Fourth Amendment deals with protecting our privacy, but how it applies to our "always-on" digital lives is a matter still to be settled. Every time you *like*, *share,* or *save* something online, that's another scrap of data (and metadata) logged and stored about you and your affiliates. These tiny dots of information—akin to a Seurat painting—cumulatively paint a picture of your activities and associations, which may be used, sold, or hacked. The daily, cumulative harvesting of data, from the latte you ordered with the swipe of your thumb to lab results (revealing a potentially damning preexisting condition), also paints a socioeconomic portrait of you, down to your DNA.

Laws are vague, elastic, or in flux, so the rights we take for granted are still up for grabs. Translating the rights outlined in the Constitution into practice for a shareable digital format leaves those rights open to interpretation.

What's a responsible and digitally dependent citizen to do? Learn how to guard your perimeter and stand up for your rights as you cross both physical and digital boundaries. Rather than throw up our hands in frustration and bemoan our inability to outrun or outsmart technocracy, we're here to help you learn and to share what works in true DIY spirit.

One key to living free is to protect yourself and your loved ones from unauthorized surveillance, marketers harvesting and reselling data from your online movements, and border agents denying you entry into the country you love.

This chapter showcases digital privacy tactics that you can begin to implement at home, at the border, and across your heavily surveilled digital existence to provide enhanced security and peace of mind. Most of these tools are free and available to the public. That is, as long as we protect net neutrality (the idea that internet service providers—ISPs—should treat all data that travels over their networks fairly, without improper discrimination in favor of particular apps, sites, or services—the foundation of the open internet. We also outline why protecting yourself matters, and what you stand to lose if you don't pay attention.

With net neutrality on the line still, freedom of information at risk, and the latest in spyware surveilling and documenting our daily transactions, look to this chapter to explain the following:

- How the Constitution applies to search, seizure, surveillance, and detainment today, especially in regard to your digital devices

- How to set up secure networks and tools to protect your digital privacy every day

- How to create stronger digital boundaries at home and the extra steps you need to take when crossing the border

- How to scan terms of service agreements for sites and apps to gauge where your data is going and how it's being used, so you can make decisions about how much to share

- How to balance privacy versus safety, when you set up your family for digital access, sharing, troubleshooting, and monitoring

Along the way, you'll meet a professionally paranoid software developer and a family-friendly tech expert.

FIELD NOTES
TERMS AND CONCEPTS TO KNOW

biometrics: Systems that use human physical identifiers such as fingerprints, voice, face, eyes, or DNA for identification or access purposes—for example, Touch or Face ID on the iPhone.

cloud: A term that comes from early network diagrams, in which the image of a cloud was used to indicate a large network, such as a wide area network (WAN). The cloud eventually became associated with the entire internet, and the two terms are now used synonymously. The cloud may also be used to describe specific online services, which are collectively labeled "cloud computing."

encryption: The process of converting data to an unrecognizable form. It is commonly used to protect sensitive information so that only authorized parties can view it. This includes files and storage devices, as well as data transferred over wireless networks and the internet.

geocaching: Finding a hidden object through GPS coordinates posted on a website.

geolocating: Digitally locating the geographical position of a person via their device through the internet.

Global Positioning System (GPS): A radio navigation system that allows users to determine their exact location, velocity, and time from anywhere.

Internet Protocol (IP) address: A unique marker used to identify a device by other systems connected via internet protocol.

internet service provider (ISP): A company that delivers internet services to consumers and/or enterprise customers. ISPs can include phone companies, like AT&T; cable companies, like Comcast; and satellite companies, like Dish Network.

malware: A malicious software program that is propagated by legitimate-seeming emails and websites designed to trick someone into downloading the program.

net neutrality: The idea that ISPs should treat all data that travels over their networks fairly, without improper discrimination in favor of or against particular companies and their apps, sites, or services. Net neutrality is founded on the principle that the internet has become and should be treated as a public utility.

phishing: Legitimate-seeming emails and websites that in reality come from scammers looking to capture password or payment information.

privatized internet: The rollback of the Federal Communications Commission's (FCC) Open Internet Order, therefore diminishing net neutrality rules, meant the loss of the ability to prevent ISPs from controlling the quality of your access to services and devices that rely on an internet connection. If ISPs control access and quality, especially based on who pays them or to favor their own subsidiaries, we will have a privatized internet.

ransomware: A type of malware that blocks you from accessing your own computer or certain files (often encrypting them without your permission or knowledge) unless you pay a ransom.

terms of service (TOS): Rules that a user must agree to in order to use a service or website. They also typically include a disclaimer (in fine print) regarding the use of data and content, which users need to be aware of in case of improper data transfer by the host website.

two-factor authentication (2FA): A security process by which the user provides two authentication factors to verify they are who they say they are, one of them typically being a user password.

THE CONSTITUTION AND SEARCH, SEIZURE, AND SURVEILLANCE

Know the Fourth

The Fourth Amendment protects us from intrusions into our private sphere, defined as both personal spaces and objects. The law holds that "the right of the people to be secure in their persons, houses, papers, and effects, against unreasonable searches and seizures, shall not be violated, and no warrants shall issue, but upon probable cause, supported by oath or affirmation, and particularly describing the place to be searched, and the persons or things to be seized."

Police and other law enforcement officials must be able to explain their actions and show that they followed protocol. We can't guarantee that the letter of the law is upheld in every instance, but it helps to understand your rights so you, with your lawyer, can challenge an unwarranted search and seizure.

Private Practice

Law enforcement can pursue a reasonable search and even detain an individual if they have a warrant or probable cause. Avoid carrying anything you wouldn't want the police, ICE, FBI, or a customs officer to see. Remember that probable cause is less difficult to prove if you are in your car than at home.

Beware of Stop and Frisk

If you are a person of color, know your rights and learn about your options. Black and brown people are disproportionately targeted due to implicit bias and racial profiling. Contact your local ACLU for details.

Terry v. Ohio

This decision (1968) allows law enforcement to search for weapons. To perform a frisk, the officer must have reasonable suspicion that an individual is armed.

To search someone and their belongings, the officer must have probable cause (i.e., he felt a knife or a gun while frisking them).

Don't Get ICE'd

U.S. Immigration and Customs Enforcement (ICE) uses what they call a "detainer" or "hold" to capture people they come in contact with via local and state law enforcement agencies. It's a common way to take immigrants into custody before beginning the deportation process. ICE can request that individuals be held in jail or at other law enforcement facilities for up to forty-eight hours before deciding whether to transfer them into the federal deportation process.

DIGITAL SECURITY AT HOME, ON THE GO, AND ABROAD

Yesterday's activists may have met in secret in church basements with Xeroxed marching orders but today we organize online—sometimes with like-minded allies whom we don't even know in real life. You may use digital platforms and tools to voice your political and ethical perspectives, from sharing news items via email list to opining on social media. Digital security is critical to protect your identity, communications, and finances. If you're also a protestor—online or off—you should be aware of some best practices and strategies for using digital tools to communicate, organize, and mobilize securely in this evolving, heavily surveilled landscape.

The level in which you lock things down is up to you: Dial it up or down per your paranoia barometer. That said, here are some DIY hacks and principles for preparing and protecting your digital communications, along with "get it done now" advice from expert Dan Treiman on specific actions to improve your privacy hygiene daily.

SAFEGUARD YOUR DATA AND YOUR DEVICES

Encryption. Encrypt data, files, and communications regularly. Don't encrypt only the content you feel could be a risk . . . that's a big red flag.

Anonymity. Use tools that allow you to remain anonymous as you email, chat, and search the internet. You can even set up your own secure browsing and network solution leveraging tools like the Tor network solution (aka the Onion Router) that allow you to mask and encrypt traffic as it travels across different servers. If this is too ambitious, there are tools that can protect your email, chat, text, browsing, search, and messaging histories.

Strong passwords. Build better passwords. Are you someone who uses *admin* or *1234* or even *password* as their passwords? Don't do that. If your OS or browser auto-suggests long and strong passwords, use them. Don't use the same password for every site. It may sound counterintuitive, but keeping passwords securely stored is a good strategy. You're more likely to get hacked outside the home than in it. Bonus tip: Disable biometric access on devices (e.g., Touch ID and Face ID) before heading out to any situation where you might encounter law enforcement, including the TSA.

Presenting a blank slate. Your computer and mobile devices are a treasure trove of information: where you've been, who you've been talking to, and what you've been researching. They transmit your individually identifiable IP address. They record where and when photos are taken. They communicate your interests via your search records and group memberships. They record who you associate with in text, email, and on Facebook. Before you attend a protest, travel across our border, or even attend a meeting, consider clearing out these troves. For example, you can clear your browser cache to get rid of recent search and site visit history. You can clear your Activity Log on Facebook. You can upload sensitive documents or save reference web pages to a secure, cloud-based storage solution, and then clear them off your device. You can then access those items from anywhere and carry less information on your device.

⬡ TOOLS FOR THE TASK

Secure Search/Messaging/Texting/Browing

Ixquick, DuckDuckGo, Wire, Signal, Jitsi, Cypher, Epic, Comodo Dragon, Brave, HTTPS Everywhere, Tor Messenger.

Secure Cloud Storage

Back Blaze, Tresorit

Encryption

For Macs, the open source GPG Suite is a collection of tools allowing you to encrypt and decrypt emails using PGP (Pretty Good Privacy) and manage your keychains on the Mac OS. Widely used by netizens of the dark web, GPG is a necessity if you communicate with Tor. For PC users, the equivalent version is GnuPG. Use web-based tool Cyph for encrypted file transfer and video chat.

Lighten your load. You don't need to bring every digital device you own to the protest or across the border. Consider getting a temporary device (aka a "burner"), disconnected from all your networks but that still allows you to document experiences, make emergency calls, and post online. You can also lighten your digital load by deleting all but the most essential apps from your mobile devices. Simply reload them later.

SAFEGUARD YOUR RELATIONSHIPS

Vet your network. Before sharing from a source, before joining a meeting, before rallying troops, take a moment to determine your comfort level with that source, the meeting organizers, or troops you're rallying. Do you need to know everyone in your protest network in real life? Perhaps not. Anonymous—the international network of hacktivists involved in anti-cyber surveillance and more—was born at the 4chan image board. Anyone can join, but elite hackers rise and collectivize in private chatrooms to enact social justice. Many post "anonymously," so if captured, they can't reveal their allies. If you're moderating access to a secret online group and don't want to go that far, protect yourself and your fellow members by vetting people who request to join, especially if they haven't been recommended by a known member. Check their social media and LinkedIn profiles and do a general search. Don't review only what they post, but how far back their online record goes. By now most people have an online record going back years.

Public posting is not secure. Think very carefully about what you post (and text), as media outlets now include screen captures of posted tweets, social posts, and even direct messages from people profiled in news stories. Discuss the preferences of your protest companions before heading out, so there are ground rules about whether or not to tag them in posts or photos. They may be affiliated with your mission but not want to be "outed" on social media.

Consider the value of in-person meeting. The most secure method of communication is face-to-face, without digital devices. Never underestimate the value of actual face time.

WHEN YOU'RE ON THE MOVE

Minimize your digital footprint. In addition to not carrying more devices than needed, or even carrying a temporary device when out in the field, minimize what can be seen on whatever devices you do carry. Log out of all your social channels and set your privacy settings so that posts aren't viewable to the public (and aren't visible to authorities if you're detained!). Turn off automated geolocation data attached to photos or included in public shares you make. Power off devices until absolutely needed to avoid a variety of high-tech hacks and surveillance techniques. (Bonus: Powering down saves battery life!)

Document with care. Pointing a digital device at a law enforcement officer can escalate the situation. When you document an event, be careful and stealthy. Don't call unnecessary attention to yourself.

WHEN YOU'RE AT THE BORDER

Between post-9/11 and Patriot Act policies and assorted implemented and threatened travel bans, traveling across the U.S. border has never been more fraught. Our first recommendation is to live a more secure digital life every day. Adopt as many of these digital privacy and security tactics as you can. Here are some additional steps to help you go through customs as smoothly as possible, even if you're a rabble-rousing part-time revolutionary.

Know thyself. Remember, your digital footprint, rap sheet, and travel history follows you everywhere. If you travel frequently overseas, especially in countries known for terrorism or sex and drug trafficking, you may be pulled aside for additional screening. From there, the plot thickens. "Secondary scrutiny" conducted by the Interagency Border Inspection System (IBIS) is the right arm of Customs and Border Protection (CBP) and can capture a more detailed digital record of you. IBIS collects and stores data on all persons leaving and entering the United States, including police records, wanted persons, stolen vehicles, and previous investigations. The CBP states that this information "is strictly used for preventing and combating terrorism and serious criminal offenses . . . to protect our nation's borders through threat analysis." If you have a travel record or affiliations with any groups that the government finds "interesting," it's probably a good idea to assume they're watching you more closely.

Know your rights. Danielle Rizzo of the American Immigration Lawyers Association says, "the Fourth Amendment (protecting against searches and seizures without probable cause or reasonable suspicion) doesn't apply in the same way at the border." U.S. citizens or noncitizens can be pulled aside without the full protections of the Fourth. If you're a U.S. citizen, you have a right to an attorney, according to the ACLU, but the CBP can search your laptop or devices whether you're a citizen or a green card holder under certain circumstances, including if you've visited countries listed in the current travel ban, your name matches the name of a person of interest on the CBP/IBIS database, or your travel documents are incomplete.

Treat TSA like any other law enforcement. It's a good idea to review the "Getting Arrested" guidelines starting on page 33. All the same guidance applies. Remember TSA, unlike other law enforcement agencies, can flag you for heightened security during future travel. So be aware of that risk.

Reporting Trouble at the U.S. Border

Even if you follow these guidelines, we can't guarantee that law enforcement will follow the rules or won't use excessive force. If you feel that your rights have been violated in any context with law enforcement, contact the ACLU. If you're mistreated at the U.S. border, specifically, you can also turn to these resources:

- File a complaint with Customs and Border Protection: https://help.cbp.gov/app/forms/complaint

- File a complaint with the Department of Homeland Security's Office for Civil Rights and Civil Liberties: https://www.dhs.gov/file-civil-rights-complaint

- If you are singled out for secondary screening multiple times over the course of several international trips, you or someone with a similar name may be on a government watch list, making you a target. If you suspect either case to be true, you can seek help from the DHS Traveler Redress Inquiry Program (TRIP): https://www.dhs.gov/dhs-trip

PROTECTING YOURSELF IN THE UNITED STATES AS A NONCITIZEN

HAVE YOU BEEN QUESTIONED ABOUT YOUR STATUS AND ARE YOU FACING POSSIBLE DETAINMENT?

You have the right to remain silent if you are being detained by police or immigration agents. There are different rules for border agents and airport personnel, as well as for people traveling on business and immigration visas. Check with a lawyer to ensure you know your status and the protocol in advance.

ARE YOU A LEGAL, DOCUMENTED IMMIGRANT?

Carry the necessary documents you need to show evidence of your status. Keep copies of all paperwork in a safe space. Make a legal plan with friends and family in case you're detained.

DO YOU HAVE YOUR PAPERS?

You must show them to immigration agents when requested. Refrain from discussing your status with anyone except your lawyer. Read everything carefully, request an interpreter if you need one, and avoid signing documents without counsel.

ARE YOU A PERMANENT RESIDENT OR GREEN CARD HOLDER?

Carry your card and keep a copy of it in a safe place. Tell a trusted friend where to find it. Renew your card at least six months before expiration.

ARE YOU A "LEGAL" RESIDENT (WITHOUT A GREEN CARD)?

Keep your employment authorization, I-94 card, passport with entry stamp, or other proof of status on hand.

Following President Trump's executive order targeting refugees and noncitizens, and the impending repeal of Deferred Action for Childhood Arrivals (DACA) program, it is more important than ever for noncitizens to know how protect themselves inside the United States.

ARE YOU A NONCITIZEN WITH A CRIMINAL HISTORY?

Save money to prepare for potential release on bond. Make arrangements with a lawyer and prepare power-of-attorney documents for dependents.

HAS AN IMMIGRATION AGENT SHOWED UP AT YOUR HOME?

You are not obligated to provide entry into your home unless agents possess a specific warrant. The ACLU advises that you "ask the officer to slip the warrant under the door or hold it up to the window." You have the right to remain silent, ask for a lawyer, and ask to make a phone call if arrested.

HAVE YOU BEEN IN THE UNITED STATES FOR TEN YEARS OR LONGER WITHOUT A CRIMINAL HISTORY?

Can you document that your U.S. citizen family members will endure excessive hardship without you? Talk to an attorney to confirm that you're eligible for cancellation of removal (a form of relief from deportation if you have been placed in a removal process). Prepare to pay a bond for release.

ARE YOU UNDOCUMENTED?

It will worsen your situation if you lie or give officials fake or forged documents. Prepare a power-of-attorney plan for dependents. Have your attorney's phone number memorized.

HAVE YOU HAD PREVIOUS ORDERS FOR DEPORTATION?

If you've never left the country but have received an order for deportation, connect with an attorney to discuss your options. If you've returned to the United States after receiving an order for deportation, you may be prosecuted. You might face up to five years in prison if your deportation was connected to a prior conviction.

Daniel Treiman's Four Tips

Daniel Treiman is a software engineer who has thought a lot about digital security while working at such companies as Google and YouTube. We asked him what a regular person (who may or may not be as tech-savvy as he) should do to protect their privacy on their home networks and devices, to keep those nefarious hackers at bay:

YOUR WI-FI ROUTER SETTINGS

- **Enable WPA2 security.** WPA protects Wi-Fi traffic from eavesdropping. Developers are continuously improving it, so use the newest version that your router offers.

- **Change the admin password.** Most routers come out of the box with a predictable admin password (like *admin*).

- **Disable Wi-Fi Protected Setup (WPS).** WPS can be exploited by hackers to gain admin access to most routers.

YOUR COMPUTER(S)

- **Always install the latest manufacturer software updates.** Most cyberattacks exploit holes that have already been patched and affect only users who haven't updated.

- **Back up your data in the cloud.** Doing so keeps your data safe from theft, hard drive failure, or ransomware attacks.

- **Encrypt whenever possible.** Enable whole-disk encryption if your computer supports it.

WEB BROWSERS

- **Look for HTTPS.** Be suspicious of any website whose URL doesn't start with *https://* (rather than plain old *http://*). Most browsers show when a site doesn't offer this secure connection (usually with a broken lock icon or a red color tint to the left of the URL in your browser bar).

- **Beware of links.** If a link triggers a download, and you aren't sure what the downloaded file is, do not open or double-click on it.

- **Install security extensions.** Common examples include HTTPS Everywhere and Web of Trust.

- **Enable two-factor authentication (2FA).** For any services that store personal information, especially email, social networks, and banking.

MOBILE DEVICES

- **Lock it up.** Lock your phone with a security PIN.

- **Encrypt here too.** Encrypt storage if your device supports it.

- **Enable remote location tracking and erasing.** This is called Find My iPhone on the iPhone and Find My Device on Android devices. If your phone is lost or stolen, it enables you to find it, to add an emergency message to whomever finds it, and to wipe it and reset it to factory settings, if necessary.

- **Beware of public Wi-Fi:** Don't use public Wi-Fi networks for anything sensitive. People can easily eavesdrop on your activity on public Wi-Fi.

TERMS OF SERVICE AND PRIVACY POLICIES:
KNOW WHERE YOUR DATA GOES

Every website, every mobile app, and every piece of software you download comes with terms of service (or terms of use) and probably a privacy policy as well. These policies are often lengthy, filled with legal jargon, and widely ignored. Company terms are often designed for the most extreme use cases and to maximize the company's rights. Services include everything they could ever want to do in these policies, even if they're nowhere near implementing them.

Companies can use your information for good—such as helping them speed up your login process and retrieve your payment information when you want to buy things. That information also helps them make personalized recommendations based on what they know about you. Not all data usage is bad. However, your data may also be used for profit and power, and companies try to give themselves a ton of leeway in how they use your data, regardless of purpose.

All that said, you may be aghast at the liberties a service can take with your data, identity, and information, yet still feel compelled to keep using that service. This can occur when the service is fundamental to your everyday life—such as your cell phone service. Even so, we recommend you be aware of what services are doing (at the very least) and that you take advantage of the ability to control the flow of your data when and where you can.

Here's a basic primer on what to look for and what kind of settings may be more easily changed to protect you. In the following cases, "they," "them," or "their" refers to the company behind the website, mobile app, service, or software program that you use.

Look for What information does a website, mobile app, service, or software program collect while you're using it—your identifying info? Your actions/activities? Your friends? Your payment information? **Why it matters** The more they collect, the more they can sell—and the more at risk you are if they suffer a data breach.

Look for How do they use the information they collect? Keep an eye on how broadly they can leverage your info to "improve their services" and target you with advertising. **Why it matters** Facebook used the "to improve our service" justification for involving live users in a sort of social experiment, manipulating what they saw in their news feeds to determine if the company could change users' emotions expressed on the platform. Pretty creepy stuff. Remember, some platforms control who and what you see, not just what you share.

Look for Who do they give your information to—their own subsidiaries? Advertising and web analytics companies? Third parties? Check whether you can opt out of some of this sharing, especially with third parties and ad-tracking companies. For that matter, what happens if the company in question gets bought? How do these rights—and your information—transfer? Do you get notified? **Why it matters** Your data may end up traveling much further than you anticipated when you signed up. Containing data transfer as much as possible mitigates your risks.

Look for How long do they store your information? You may be surprised to know that even when you delete your account altogether, a service may store your information. This can last for years, and sometimes forever. **Why it matters** Knowing how long your information gets stored makes you take it even more seriously before posting, right?

Look for Can they monetize it? Yes, they're probably running ads, but are they also using your information to target the ad, and can you adjust the advertising you see? You should check whether they mention selling your data (typically in aggregate, not necessarily individually identifiable, but still . . .). **Why it matters** It's reasonable to think about the value exchange. If they are making money off your data, do you feel like you are getting enough value in exchange?

Look for Do they own your comments or other content you may publish on their platform (tweets, photos, and so on)? **Why it matters** You may own your own posted content, from comments to photos and more, but look for whether posting it in the app or on the platform grants them a license to reuse your content. And for what? Is it just for marketing and promotion purposes, or for anything they want without limit? Again, there may not be cases of platforms taking users' photos and selling the work, but their terms may very well give them the right to do so. Better to know before you post.

Look for Do they track you once you leave their sites? Look for a section about "cookies," small pieces of data sent from a site you're visiting to your computer that are then stored on your computer. **Why it matters** A cookie enables a company to track you on their site and beyond. Cookies explain how you may see ads for products you checked out on one site show up on a totally different site. You can disable (or clear) cookies at the browser level. Or you can take a less drastic approach and disable cookies for a particular app or site or service. The trade-off is that sites and services won't work as well (or sometimes at all) if you disable cookies.

Look for What are their obligations to alert you to changes in policy? Usually there is a section of the terms that specifically calls out "Changes to Terms of Use." Can they make changes any time they want, effective immediately? Do you have the chance to review and make a decision on whether to continue using the service? **Why it matters** If a service has the right to change policies whenever they want without notification, you may want to schedule regular reviews of your settings and their policies to make sure nothing has changed to the degree that you no longer want to use the service.

Look for What are their obligations to alert you should law enforcement request your data (and if they provide it)? Do they require warrants or subpoenas, or just maintain a good faith belief that law enforcement needs the information? Will they notify you? **Why it matters** The answers may be a little unsettling. Many services don't require a subpoena and won't alert you.

Look for What are your options if there is a breach involving your data? (For example, can you sue?) **Why it matters** Many services build in a requirement to resolve disputes via arbitration rather than handling it in the courts.

Additional terms to check for when downloading and using apps for the first time:

- Is location tracking on? Can you turn it off, or set it to be on only when you open the app, rather than running in the background?
- Are push notifications on? Can you control their frequency?
- Is access to the camera or microphone turned on? Is it always on, or only when using the app?

Here are two additional ways to check what permissions you've already given across your device and services:

Check your settings. Notifications and Privacy are two subsections in your mobile phone's top-level settings where you can review what you've currently agreed to, app by app. Similarly, your computer's operating system and browser should allow you to set privacy preferences. Check out the preferences for your preferred browser, for cookies, location sharing, and more. Finally, individual platforms like Facebook have extensive settings areas where you can check similar location-tracking and other privacy settings. Don't assume the default settings reflect the permissions you prefer—and don't assume that companies never change those defaults. Sometimes they change without notice. Audit your privacy settings on all your social media platforms frequently.

Use a service. Maybe you gave an app permission once to take a silly quiz like all your friends, but you didn't mean for the app to still track your every move three years later. MyPermissions is one service that can tell you which platforms are currently accessing your data on mobile devices. It will also help you remove or adjust those permissions. In addition, you can go to your Facebook settings directly and click on Apps to edit or simply turn *off* apps, websites, and games from having access to your data.

If you are like the average person who now juggles multiple devices and even more apps, platforms, tools, and services across those devices, it's likely that you will continue to have vulnerabilities. Controlling what you can, as much as you can, is recommended nonetheless.

HOW TO SET UP YOUR KIDS OR PARENTS TO GIVE YOU ACCESS
BUT PROTECT THEM FROM SURVEILLANCE

For those of us in the "Sandwich Generation," dealing with two very different generations of tech users in our families can be challenging. Our kids are digital natives, but they still need guidance, parameters, and careful oversight. Our parents came to technology later in life, but they're adopting new tools at a rapid pace. While the boomer and senior generations may be comfortable users of technology, they are not always comfortable troubleshooting their devices. How can you provide all the right support, efficiently, and without exposing either your kids or your parents to security holes?

To navigate the complexities, we enlisted Carley Knobloch, a personal tech expert who regularly appears on the *Today* show and HGTV.com, to deliver sage advice on technology practices for the whole family. Carley has tested and used a wide variety of solutions and shares her favorite tools (and her philosophy).

THE BIG TRADE-OFF: SAFETY VERSUS PRIVACY

When it comes to school-age kids, safety is more important than privacy. As kids get older and closer to adulthood, parents can grant more responsibility and more privacy. Carley makes this analogy: "Having access to the internet is a bit like giving your kid a chef's knife—at some point, they're too young for it entirely. Then there's the middle period, where they should have exposure to it and begin some supervised use—because ultimately, before they live on their own, you want them to know how to chop an onion! Same thing with the internet: an equally useful tool that has a double edge and can be potentially harmful."

In practice, erring on the side of caution means parents should get *allll* the passwords. And you need to use those passwords to check up on your kids occasionally. There also need to be consequences if you discover your kid has tried to block you or change their password or set up alternate accounts. It will likely happen—so be prepared.

Carley's philosophy: "Make sure your kids act in a way where they continue to earn the privilege of having access to the internet. Many parents are too worried about being 'cool' with their kids and turn a blind eye to the potential harms that can come from unsupervised internet time."

With older parents, you're dealing with grown people who can make their own decisions—the pendulum needs to swing far more definitively toward honoring privacy. You want access to their devices to help them troubleshoot or keep everything updated and secure, which means you have their passwords; but it's probably inappropriate for you to be able to access their devices at any time without their explicit consent. Look for tools that give your parents control over when you have access (see "Tools for the Task" below).

Safety can also be an issue when it comes to your parents. Carley suggests investing in a whole new world of smart-home technologies that get the safety-versus-privacy equation right: "There are many smart sensors that don't have cameras (which would be an invasion of privacy) but will alert an adult child if, say, their parent hasn't opened the fridge in twenty-four hours or descended the stairs. It's all about compromise—not supervision, but oversight and regular check-ins. Also, new health trackers can monitor a medicine regimen as well as vital signs—data can be sent to a physician or an adult in charge of care."

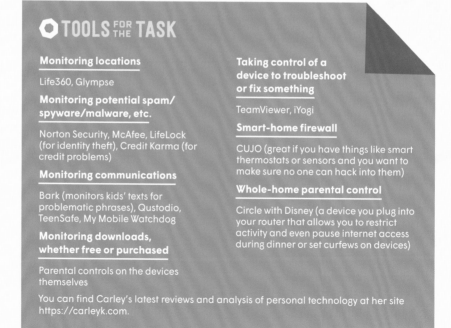

⬡ TOOLS FOR THE TASK

Monitoring locations

Life360, Glympse

Monitoring potential spam/spyware/malware, etc.

Norton Security, McAfee, LifeLock (for identity theft), Credit Karma (for credit problems)

Monitoring communications

Bark (monitors kids' texts for problematic phrases), Qustodio, TeenSafe, My Mobile Watchdog

Monitoring downloads, whether free or purchased

Parental controls on the devices themselves

Taking control of a device to troubleshoot or fix something

TeamViewer, iYogi

Smart-home firewall

CUJO (great if you have things like smart thermostats or sensors and you want to make sure no one can hack into them)

Whole-home parental control

Circle with Disney (a device you plug into your router that allows you to restrict activity and even pause internet access during dinner or set curfews on devices)

You can find Carley's latest reviews and analysis of personal technology at her site https://carleyk.com.

DISCLOSURE IS KEY

Whether dealing with parents or kids, Carley recommends full disclosure.

For kids: "Starting on the day you hand them a smartphone, the dynamic should be that 'This is a device I paid for, and I will loan it to you if you continue to meet the requirements for using one.' Let them know what the rules are. When I hear parents lament about their kids being on the phone at dinner or other inappropriate places, I don't often hear them talk about how earning use of the smartphone is ongoing. I sound like a hard-ass, but I would argue that this dynamic is positive—it shifts control to the kids. If they don't do what's required, they lose the right to continued use. It's all in their court."

For parents: "Of course, with parents, it's totally different—they are adults who need help and guidance, not monitoring and teaching. Keeping an open dialogue and setting up a regular maintenance schedule cuts back on problems. I've also found that keeping a diary of what went wrong with their technology and how to fix it is helpful, so that they can become more independent."

WHAT YOU'RE LOOKING FOR WHEN MONITORING

For kids: "It's about content filtering, and tracking and monitoring communications (to check for concerning words or phrases, and so on). My (immediate) family uses a location tracker called Life360 so that we can see one another's whereabouts at all times. All of us—even me and my husband! We don't feel like it's an invasion of privacy, but other families might feel differently."

For parents: "It's more about organizing things for access in an emergency, having remote access to troubleshoot and fix tech issues, and making sure devices are clear of malware, spyware, viruses, and other problematic downloads. Depending on your parents' age and health, you may want to add health-monitoring tools to the mix, and ultimately you might want to add your parents to a location-tracking tool like Life360 too, especially if they live elsewhere or in a flood or fire zone."

TAKEAWAYS AND RESOURCES

It's a brave new world, online and off, so here are some ways to make it less vulnerable.

There Are Trade-Offs

If you use the internet and mobile devices, you sign terms of service and make yourself more vulnerable to hacking and surveillance. Assess the trade-offs and make your own decisions about which risks are reasonable and come with enough benefit.

Know Your Rights

Start by knowing your rights. You have rights if being detained or arrested. You have rights at home or at the border. Commit these to memory, but keep a copy of them in your wallet just in case memory fails, using some of the handy tools shared in this chapter.

Protect Your Data

Mitigate risk by bringing fewer digital devices to the border or to a protest, privatizing your social channels, putting pertinent data and information in the cloud, and encrypting. Use all the tools at your disposal to make your data less accessible—both to the government and to hackers.

Risky Business

Protection is even more important if you are a firebrand, a gadfly, a rabble-rouser, or a change agent. Could you be a person of interest to the powers that be? Be honest about what's on the other side of your baseball card . . . like if you've got an arrest record, for example. The more at risk you are, the more you should transition to using the secure tools we list in this chapter.

Support a Fair, Free Internet

If net neutrality is overturned in full and the internet is privatized, your fair, free access to information could be hampered. Keep your eyes on this issue and let your elected officials know you support net neutrality.

RESOURCE LINKS

The TechTerms Online Dictionary
https://techterms.com

The EFF on Net Neutrality
https://www.eff.org/issues/
net-neutrality

EFF Border Search Pocket Guide
https://www.eff.org/document/
eff-border-search-pocket-guide

Miranda Rights
www.mirandarights.org

**Customs and Border Protection
Complaint**
https://help.cbp.gov/app/forms/
complaint

**Department of Homeland
Security Traveler Redress Inquiry
Program (TRIP)**
https://www.dhs.gov/dhs-trip

**Filing a Freedom of Information Act
(FOIA) Request**
https://www.bettergov.org/
node/1379346

**CNN: Can They Search My Phone?
A Guide to Your Rights at the Border**
http://www.cnn.com/2017/02/16/us/
border-legal-rights-faq-trnd/index.html

**U.S. Customs and Border Patrol:
CBP Search Authority**
https://www.cbp.gov/travel/
cbp-search-authority

**Ultraculture's review of secure
Internet tools**
https://ultraculture.org/blog/2016/
01/10/private-browsing

MyPermissions Privacy Cleaner
https://mypermissions.com

**Tech World's Best Secure
Browsers of 2017**
https://www.techworld.com/security/
best-8-secure-browsers-3246550

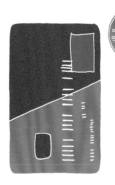

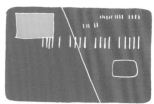

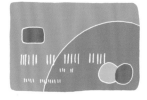

3

ECONOMIC PRESSURE

Journalist and anti-lynching activist Ida B. Wells-Barnett stated "the appeal to the white man's pocket has ever been more effectual than all the appeals ever made to his conscience." This idea has been verified frequently, in many rights, justice, and labor movements involving economic action.

This chapter examines boycotts, divestment, and other economic tactics. We introduce the concept of "buycotts" to help you strategically spend and invest your money to help instead of hurt. We'll uplift the reality that reputation is a valuable form of currency.

During a time when social media, corporate social-responsibility programs, and relationship-driven marketing influence how people feel about brands, most companies want to be in good standing with the public. That's why we explore both traditional and innovative methods to apply economic pressure on companies, governments, and other entities possessing social power.

Whether we like it or not, money drives governments, political campaigns, for-profit and nonprofit organizations, and media. It determines who has privilege and power in society and whose ideas, interests, and communities get left out of public discourse and private decision-making. That's why we explore how we can use our collective strengths and diverse resources (monetary, people-power, consumer status, and otherwise) to inspire institutions to embrace practices, policies, and partnerships to best serve the public.

Refer to this chapter to learn about:

- Boycotts and divestments

- Buycotts and how to spend your money wisely

- The power of shareholder advocacy

- How to use economic pressure to take down an oppressor

- How to get your workplace to change/expand corporate policies

Again, as Gloria Steinem said, "We can tell our values by looking at our checkbook stubs." Throughout this chapter, you'll hear how economic pressure ignites change. No matter how much each of us has to spend, the choices we make about how we use the power of our purse can build a better present and future for all of us.

FIELD NOTES
TERMS AND CONCEPTS TO KNOW

boycott: An individual or group decision to refrain from purchasing services or goods from a company, organization, or nation as a form of protest and resistance. This term originated in the nineteenth century when Irish land agent Charles C. Boycott denied calls to lower tenant farmers' rent. In response, his community refused to work with him and left his crops untended.

buycott: An individual or group decision to intentionally purchase services or goods from a company, organization, particular demographic, or nation as a form of support for their practices or policies. Buycotts are often sparked as an act of solidarity to help sustain businesses that opposing groups are boycotting. While buycotts have been used to drive purchasing toward companies, a common ongoing buycott approach is to favor purchasing from groups, such as small businesses, Black-owned businesses, or women-owned businesses. A play on the term *boycott*.

shareholder advocacy: Activists from diverse social justice movements have used public awareness campaigns, grassroots organizing, and other tactics to successfully organize shareholder activists to raise their voices and ask public companies to take action on issues. This tactic was used in recent years to push for divestment to end apartheid in South Africa, to stop the use of fossil fuels, and to build support for marriage equality in the United States.

shareholder resolutions: Each year, shareholders of publicly held companies may present proposals during a corporation's annual shareholders meeting. These recommendations can involve a range of matters, including structure and governance practices and policies, election spending and lobbying, corporate social responsibility programs, labor rights, and fiscal issues. The Securities and Exchange Commission (SEC) oversees how such proposals and resolutions are managed nationwide.

BOYCOTTS, BUYCOTTS, DIVESTMENTS
SPENDING YOUR MONEY WISELY

Simply put, money is power. That's why boycotts, values-based purchasing (also known as buycotts), and divestment movements became a part of our human story when we started trading and selling centuries ago.

Ever since the Meccan boycott of the Hashemites in the year 617 BC, people around the world have used economic sanctions to put social pressure on business owners, government officials, decision makers, and institutions. Although we wish that more companies would put people over profits, U.S. public companies often operate on the rarely questioned assumption that they're required to prioritize shareholder value over everything else. We could spend time trying to convince them that this is not actually a corporate or legal requirement, but history has proven that financial loss due to consumer activism often yields swifter results than appeals to consciences.

Movements powered by these tactics are informed by that history and the principle that corporate leaders, advertisers, and investors are more compelled to listen, transform policy, and take action when their profits are on the line. If you're considering using economic pressure as a tool, it's important to determine the right strategic approach for your goals. There's a myriad of ways to vote with your wallet. Here are some pro tips:

BOYCOTTS

When a person or group of people elect not to spend their resources on goods, amenities, and services from a company that misses a moral and/or ethical mark, they are participating in a primary boycott. If you also decide not to spend your hard-earned cash at an establishment that sells those goods, amenities, and services, that's a secondary boycott.

BUYCOTTS

Alternatively, buycotts are campaigns where people intentionally purchase from a company whose politics and policies they support. These actions often happen as a counterprotest to boycotts organized by opposition groups. Nearly every brand that President Trump has activated against via his Twitter account has experienced a surge in new customers. It has happened for brands big (*Vanity Fair* magazine, Nordstrom) and small (Penzeys Spices, the owner of which started posting long *#resistance*-themed missives on Facebook and saw sales and new customers increase significantly in response). Buycotts can also emerge in support of marginalized groups and communities who are targeted. For example, New Yorkers organized to support Muslim taxi drivers and bodega owners in the midst of the Trump administration's discriminatory travel ban.

DIVESTMENT OR DIVESTITURE

Divestment or divestiture campaigns are defined as the opposite of an investment. Popularized during the anti-apartheid movement in the 1980s, calls for divestment have erupted on college campuses on a regular basis for almost forty years. Presently, sanction campaigns like these are fought on campuses nationwide in support of climate justice, prison abolition, fossil fuels, and more.

MAKE A PLAN

Once you've decided which tactic you want to use, identify whom you're targeting, what their pain points are, and whose support they rely on to maintain their bottom line. In most cases, this includes identifying prominent individuals or aligned influencers, advertisers, investors, the media, and key consumer demographics. If you're campaigning against a company, research who has the most power to give you what you want, and think about the scope, scale, and focus on the boycott or divestment action from their perspective. For example, if you're targeting a corporation, direct your communications, petitions, and demands to their board of directors or CEO. In the case of a university, materials and actions related to the sanctions should be directed at the institution's president and the board of trustees.

BUILD YOUR MOVEMENT

Keep your requests accessible and achievable for your community members. Make it easy for people to understand what you're organizing for and how they can help. Engage the press by sharing your mission statement. Keep stakeholders updated about new developments, negotiations, and actions they can join. If you're targeting advertisers or stakeholders, keep adding new targets as others start to pull their support from the company in question. Keep the momentum going until you get your demands met, or at the very least until you achieve the visibility you need to leverage policy change and build social awareness.

BE VISIBLE AND BE HEARD

Throughout your action, keep reinforcing your succinct and compelling message by issuing your rationale and your list of demands, and expanding visibility for your network of support through rallies, petitions, sit-ins, strikes, speak-outs, and social media.

SUPPLY WHAT FOLKS NEED

Rome wasn't built in a day, but sometimes people get impatient. Provide ethical options for your community to support so that a boycott is less painful. Actively promoting a buycott while engaging in a boycott is a powerful way to flex your political muscle publicly, and it helps sustain and support businesses with honorable practices.

Key Points

Economic action is effective. If you deploy it as a tactic, make it strategic, accessible, and visible.

Boycotts at a Glance

617 BC First recorded boycott: Meccan boycott of the Hashemites

1700s American Revolution boycott of British products

1891 Persian Tobacco Protest

1905 Chinese boycott of U.S. goods in response to the Chinese Exclusion Act

1919 As a part of the Swadeshi movement for Indian independence, Mahatma Gandhi and others boycotted British goods

1933 Anti-Nazi boycott of German goods

1955 Montgomery Bus Boycott

1965–70 United Farm Workers' Delano grape strike

1980 United States–led boycott of the Summer Olympics in Moscow

1980s Divestment movement against apartheid in South Africa

1984 Soviet-led boycott of the Summer Olympics in Los Angeles

1990s–2000s Divestment against genocide in Sudan's Darfur conflict

2005 Boycott, Divestment, and Sanctions movement for equality for Palestinians

2005 "Girlcott" against sexist merchandise sold at Abercrombie & Fitch

2016–present *#GrabYourWallet* boycott of retailers who do business with the Trump family

2017 Trump inauguration boycott by elected officials

2017 Boycott of Breitbart News and its advertisers, including Whole Foods and Amazon

2017 NFL boycotts both in support of and opposition to *#TakeAKnee* protests against racial inequality and police violence

TAKING DOWN AN OPPRESSOR

THE BILL O'REILLY TIMELINE

This timeline of Bill O'Reilly's epic ouster is just one example of how to handle bullies who punch down by pushing back and shining a light on the truth.

A whistle-blowing *New York Times* investigation led by Emily Steel and Michael Schmidt unearthed that longtime Fox News host Bill O'Reilly and the network had paid five women, all of whom had accused him of sexual harassment, $45 million in settlements since 2002. A grassroots movement led by organizations such as Color of Change, Media Matters for America, Women's March, UltraViolet, and others successfully pressured O'Reilly's advertisers and Fox to remove him from the airwaves.

APRIL 1, 2017

The *New York Times* reveals Bill O'Reilly's fifteen-year history of sexual harassment accusations and settlements.

APRIL 4, 2017

The Women's March team releases its digital storytelling hashtag campaign, *#DropOReilly*. They tweet, "Women, let's use the power of our voice and tell advertisers to #DropOReilly. Share your own stories of sexual harassment in the workplace." In the face of increasing pressure, up to twenty-two companies, including Hyundai, Mercedes-Benz, Mitsubishi, Sanofi, and Allstate, pulled advertising from *The O'Reilly Factor*.

APRIL 5, 2017

President Donald Trump (who is also the subject of sexual harassment claims) endorses Bill O'Reilly in an interview with the *New York Times*, describing him as "a person I know well—he is a good person . . . I don't think Bill did anything wrong." On the same day, Jenny Craig suspends their ads from *The O'Reilly Factor*.

APRIL 11, 2017

As the controversy reaches a fever pitch, O'Reilly tells viewers that he will be taking a "vacation" and shares his plan to return on April 24.

APRIL 18, 2017

Carrying a petition with 140,000 signers calling for O'Reilly to be fired, UltraViolet, a feminist group, demonstrates outside of Fox News headquarters. A new accuser comes forward on the same day, accusing O'Reilly of both racial and sexual harassment.

APRIL 10, 2017

Ad-tracking firm iSpot.tv reports that a little bit less than seven minutes of ad time was sold versus the fifteen minutes of ad time purchased a month before, as public pressure escalates.

APRIL 8, 2017

A *Saturday Night Live* sketch led by Alec Baldwin mocks Bill O'Reilly and refers to his "scandal."

APRIL 19, 2017

Bill O'Reilly is officially dismissed from Fox. The network announces that Tucker Carlson will move into the 8:00 p.m. slot.

WHAT SHAREHOLDERS CAN DO

If you scour *Forbes* and *Fortune* magazines, you might think activist shareholders are activating only to maximize shareholder value, perhaps via hostile takeovers or finding "efficiencies" (i.e., layoffs). But several decades ago a new kind of activist shareholder arose—one who wants to hold companies more accountable to doing good in the world as they make money. Activist shareholders drove the effort to divest from South Africa to protest apartheid, and more recently, they have achieved big wins in getting companies to become more responsible for environmental impact.

But what can you do as an individual? More than you think. If you rally your networks to start thinking like activist shareholders, you can be part of a movement, one share at a time.

START READING ANNUAL SHAREHOLDER REPORTS

When you hold stock in a public company of any size, you receive their annual report. The SEC defines an annual report as "a state-of-the-company report, including financial data, results of operations, market segment information, new product plans, subsidiary activities, and research and development activities on future programs. Reporting companies must send annual reports to their shareholders when they hold annual meetings to elect directors. Under the proxy rules, reporting companies are required to post their annual reports, on their company websites."

Most probably take one look at a document like this and file it away (or toss it in the recycle bin), but there's important information in that annual mailing that can inform shareholder activism. Step one: Read the annual report (which was written by the company and filtered through their PR, investor relations, and legal staff to within an inch of its life). Step two: Scour that annual mailing for items shareholders can vote on, such as changes to the board of directors and shareholder resolutions. (This information may be buried in the back of an already long and daunting document!)

THE INFLUENCE OF SHAREHOLDER RESOLUTIONS

Shareholder resolutions are brought to companies from almost any shareholders. You can own as little as the lesser of either $2,000 or 1 percent worth of stock. These resolutions aren't binding; there's no requirement for a company to act on one, whether successfully "passed" or not. But resolutions can influence a company in two ways.

First, they indicate shareholder sentiment. Public companies care very much about that because they want to avoid shareholder sell-offs or even lawsuits. The second way that resolutions influence a company is if the press learns about them and starts to cover any related controversy.

If you want to know what kind of resolutions are being voted on by shareholders from prominent companies, especially those addressing environmental, social, and governance issues (called ESG resolutions) check out https://ProxyPreview.org. Every year Proxy Preview compiles and indexes such resolutions, with a mission of helping you vote your values. The report may also give you great ideas on kinds of resolutions you can propose yourself!

If you create a resolution yourself and get it on a proxy statement, you can reach out to institutional fund managers to try to garner support from what are likely to be some of the largest shareholders.

Shareholder resolutions are presented and voted on at annual company meetings. As a shareholder at any level, you are entitled to attend that meeting. If you propose a resolution that's accepted onto the proxy statement, you (or your representative) must attend to present your proposal.

Chances are you aren't planning to attend a company's annual meeting. Nevertheless, you can "vote by proxy." The proxy statement is included in the annual mailing with the annual report, and should outline the ways to vote your proxy by mail, phone, or online. If you have a financial manager, you can instruct them to keep you apprised of resolutions and ask for your vote when delivered. Or you can give them guidelines on how you want them to vote on your behalf. Not voting (or letting your financial manager vote without guidance) is likely a vote for a course of action you don't support.

WHAT IF YOU'RE INVESTED VIA MUTUAL FUNDS, 401(K)S, OR PENSION PLANS?

If your stock holdings are all via investments in a mutual fund, 401(k), pension plan, or the like, you'll still get reports from such funds on how they're invested. You can track the individual stocks in which the fund holds positions, but you can neither propose nor vote on shareholder resolutions, as the fund itself is considered the shareholder. That doesn't mean you can't have influence though— it's just that you're trying to influence the fund managers instead. Fund managers don't always vote and may, in fact, be prone to vote with management as a matter of course. However, you can let them know how you would like them to vote (and encourage other folks to do the same). Mutual funds are required to share their policies and processes for deciding how to vote, and also to share proxy voting records.

RALLYING FELLOW SHAREHOLDERS

If you want to have more assurance that your voice gets heard on a shareholder resolution, put your social network to work. Figure out if you know other shareholders and organize them to vote. Start an online petition (see "How to Make the Most of Online Petitions," page 154), and above all, use your social media platform to amplify your position and any relevant petitions. The more folks who cosign and share your position, the more likely the media will catch wind of it. Effective modern activist shareholders use the internet and social media as tools to increase their chances of success.

Whether you want to influence executive compensation, factory working conditions, environmental practices, corporate lobbying or investment practices, or other issues, consider not only voting your values as shareholder, but leading the charge.

WHERE YOU WORK
COMPANY POLICIES AND HOW TO ADVOCATE FOR CHANGE

Your workplace may be the institution that has the most direct impact on your daily life—more so than the government. Advocating for change at your company can shift conditions for you and your coworkers, but it can also have a wider impact by setting new precedents for your industry. This guide is meant to give you ideas on how to bring change to your workplace, even if it's just one policy.

Depending on the size of the company where you work, policies and procedures may have been codified in lengthy tomes or hastily created on an as-needed basis. They may be based on standard templates downloaded from the internet, developed by consultants with a one-size-fits-all approach, or cribbed from the policies of the last place your HR manager worked. In other words, the policies may not reflect a huge amount of intellectual capital or a deep amount of emotional investment by management. If so, they are ripe for change. But where do you start to look for policies and procedures that could be updated? Here are a few ideas for institutional policies that you could tackle.

FIND YOUR COMPANY'S POLICIES AND PROCEDURES

- Start with your new-hire paperwork. What did you have to review and sign when you started? If you don't have it, ask to see the latest new-hire package.

- Employee handbooks: Does your company have one?

- The benefits package: Does your company have all its benefit information available at an online portal or in a package to review?

- If all else fails, ask your HR person, or whoever handles the logistics of hiring and terminating employees and administering company benefits.

Look for Medical benefits that indicate an outdated perspective, or even outright bias

- Is Viagra covered but not birth control? Vasectomies, but not vasectomy reversals?
- Is health coverage available only for spouses, particularly in heterosexual relationships, rather than same-sex spouses or domestic partners?
- Is infertility treatment coverage available?

Why it matters Some health coverage policies seem to have been written before there were many women in the workforce, and before it became much more common for people to be openly gay in the workplace. If your company has a diverse workforce, they may be able to serve that workforce better with a few changes to their policies.

Look for Time-off policies that indicate an outdated perspective, or even outright bias

- Can men take paternity leave?
- Is leave available for adoptions, in addition to live births?
- Is leave available for caregiving for sick relatives other than children?
- Does the company offer any alternative work schedules, for example, shifting to part-time or contractor status or job-sharing for employees who may need short- or long-term leaves, medical, maternity, caregiving, or otherwise?

Why it matters One way that women are held back in the workplace from the outset is through the assumption that they are the primary (and sometimes sole) caregiver or parent, even when they're partnered or co-parenting. Additionally, the lack of subsidized childcare policy sometimes siphons women off from the workforce after they do a cost–benefit analysis. Policies that offer men the same leave opportunities, that recognize that giving care to our parents or bonding with newly adopted children is as important as the act of recovering from childbirth, and that acknowledge that going from short-term leaves back to immediate full-time work is challenging can help equalize the priority given to all caregivers. Companies typically also benefit from retaining great employees with strong institutional knowledge ... a fact that you should make sure to point out when advocating for updated policies.

Look for Hiring and pay policies

- If the company is seeking to diversify its workforce, does it require a diverse interview panel for prospective employees?
- Are there prescribed pay bands (specifying minimum to maximum salaries) for specific job titles or levels? Are they available for any employee to review?
- Is there a stated policy that pay equity is a company goal?

Why it matters Diverse interview panels not only generate diverse perspectives on prospective employees, but they send a message to the prospective hire that the company already values a diverse workforce. Pay and benefit transparency, in general, makes it harder for inequities to be established and to widen.

Look for Telecommuting and flextime policies

- Is there a documented policy, or does it seem haphazard?
- Are employees compensated for their telecommuting expenses, such as high-speed internet at home?
- Is the policy explicitly designed to accommodate parenting-oriented off-site tasks, but not other off-site tasks a nonparent might need to take care of?

Why it matters With women still bearing most of the burden of childrearing and caregiving, telecommuting or flextime policies affect moms most. If they are the only ones who take advantage of them, the lack of face time can affect how their performance on the job is perceived, even if they are productive working remotely. There are many documented advantages to remote work, from increased productivity to lower environmental footprints, but it can be a cultural adjustment. Conversely, nonparents may feel at a disadvantage if the only flextime requests granted are related to child-rearing.

Look for Prospective and current employee review and evaluation policies

- Are employees guaranteed performance evaluations?

- Are managers trained to give actionable reviews?

- Does the company document objectives? How granular do those objectives get? Company-wide? Departmental? Individual?

- Are you entitled to update your documented individual job objectives if the company's or department's objectives change?

- Who gets access to your evaluations? Can you get access?

Why it matters Understanding how job performance is measured is great. Knowing changes outside your control won't be held against you is even better. Knowing the company's official HR position on you is great. Knowing who gets access (for example, how much a new boss is privy to) is even better.

Look for Company conflict reporting and resolution policies

- What avenues exist for reporting issues? This is especially pertinent if someone's direct manager is the one causing the issue.

- What is the policy to prevent retaliation for reporting issues?

- Are there avenues for anonymous reporting (and what are the company's policies around validating anonymous complaints)?

- Is there a clear definition of what constitutes unacceptable behavior and treatment of colleagues?

- Is there a definition of what kinds of actions would qualify as (hopefully unacceptable) retaliation?

Why it matters Having a fair, documented process to address clearly defined inappropriate behaviors without putting the reporting employee at unnecessary risk should be the gold standard for organizations.

- Start by asking questions. Don't assume you know why the policy in question is in place. Don't assume you'll encounter resistance to changing it. Start with a positive, open approach: Is the company aware of this policy or benefit? Was it defined that way purposefully, or is it a legacy or default policy? Has the company ever investigated changing it—and is there a cost involved, or a liability issue that's not immediately obvious?

- Once you understand the circumstances behind the policy, think about the levels of change that might be possible. Are there interim steps that would be helpful in the short term? Are there steps the company could take to share the cost or mitigate the liability, for example? Try to avoid a binary win-or-lose, on-or-off demand that backs the company (and you) into a corner.

- Research the policies of the most innovative competing companies. If your company has trouble filling positions with or retaining top talent because it goes to a competitor, modernizing policies could be helpful on several fronts.

- Talk to fellow employees. You're more likely to get a policy changed if you build momentum with a larger number of employees. If the subject matter is sensitive, you can conduct an anonymous survey. But do your due diligence so you have an idea of what the outcome of that survey will be. Share your concerns with colleagues. People don't necessarily have to share personal details to give you an idea of their perspective.

Pick a policy that impacts you, learn its pedigree, and go find colleagues who agree with you that change would be an improvement. That can be your sole goal or the start of process. Either way, bringing change to your own company is a great way to revolutionize the workplace.

The State of Unions and the Rise of the Freelance Worker and "Gig Economy"

The rise of unions in the early twentieth century gave all workers, even non-union workers, benefits that we take for granted today—from the concepts of a weekend, overtime pay, maternity leave, and employer-provided health benefits to the end of child labor. Thirty-odd years ago, more than 20 percent of the wage and salary workers in the United States were members of unions. However, today that number has been sliced to 10.7 percent. You'd be forgiven for not realizing this fact, given how some politicians demonize unions and their influence.

Unions have strong presence in public service, with more than a third of public sector workers unionized . . . public school teachers, police, and so on; however, only 6.4 percent of private sector workers are in unions. Another even more recent trend is the rise of what is sometimes called the "gig economy," where even large, profitable companies rely exclusively on freelance workers to deliver their primary services. While much of this approach encourages individual advocacy, there is no arguing that collective advocacy, for example the collective bargaining process of unions, is powerful.

To some, it may sound like a relic of the industrial revolution to hear about workers penalized for efforts to unionize, but as recently as November 2017 DNAinfo abruptly shut down all of its online media outlets (Gothamist, LAist, and others) when staff voted to unionize. Still, we believe in the power of collective advocacy, so if the prospect of going it alone to advocate for workplace change is too risky, here are a variety of resources to turn to for information, protection, and support:

- The AFL-CIO on how to form a union: https://aflcio.org/formaunion

- Fight for 15, an organization dedicated to raising the minimum wage: https://fightfor15.org

- Working America, an organization fighting for the rights of workers who are not unionized: https://www.workingamerica.org/about

- American Federation of Teachers: https://www.aft.org

- The Freelancer's Union: https://www.freelancersunion.org

- Retail, Wholesale and Department Store Union: http://www.rwdsu.info

- Screen Actors Guild and the American Federation of Television and Radio Artists: https://www.sagaftra.org

- The U.S. Department of Labor site specifically for wage and hourly workers: https://www.dol.gov/whd/workers.htm

- The U.S. Equal Employment Opportunity Commission (EEOC): https://www.eeoc.gov

IMPROVING A WOMEN'S COMPANY'S HEALTH-CARE COVERAGE

In 2016, women's media company SheKnows Media added a buy-in option to its health-care plan for employees to add infertility treatment coverage. By the middle of 2017, two babies were born as a result of this added option—and it all started with one new employee, Kate Durkin, who ironically had no plans to have a baby.

Her experience as the instigator of this significant change in company policy is a case study in how one person who's willing to organize with others while listening to the company perspective can change lives—and in this case, create them!

WHAT HAPPENS WHEN YOU ASSUME

Before joining SheKnows, Kate had been in the process of exploring freezing her eggs. Egg freezing follows every step of IVF (in vitro fertilization) treatment, save for the last two: fertilizing and then reinserting the eggs. Her company at the time, a start-up, offered excellent coverage, ultimately covering around $25,000 of the cost, and she hadn't thought to ask about this particular detail of health coverage when going through the interview process. In fact, she assumed that going from a start-up to an established women's media company that had a majority of women employees meant it was a given.

In her first benefits review meeting with SheKnows human resources, *after* taking the job, she discovered that she had been wrong to assume—and she was likely far from the first person to be taken by surprise.

"When you're exploring a new job, you often don't get access to such granular details about their health benefits," Kate said. "Frankly, you're unlikely to ask about infertility coverage, signaling you want to get pregnant."

She was told she was the first person to bring it up.

TAKEAWAYS AND RESOURCES

Everyday revolutionaries must be agile, creative, and open to new ways to spark change, but history and present-day movements have shown us that economic action works. Consider these takeaways to make your action visible, intentional, and reachable to the communities you need to mobilize.

Choose Your Own Adventure
Once you determine that economic action is the pathway to victory, identify which tactics will help you reach your goal most efficiently and effectively. Whether you organize a boycott, buycott, employee action, and/or a shareholder activist campaign, it's important to understand first the political economy of the entity where you're applying pressure. What hits their bottom line?

Be Like an Archer
As great feminist activist Florynce ""Flo" Kennedy once said, "Don't agonize, organize." Once you've identified the tactics you want to employ around an institution or an organization, identify your specific direct target. Do your research and discover who has the power to give you what you want, then zero in on applying pressure in that direction.

Be Solution-Driven
Envision myriad solutions when bringing a problem to light. Although it's not your responsibility to fix any-one else's mess, providing a vision for a productive pathway or progress is a way to shut down attempts at derail-ing, dismissing, and shaming. It's also a great way to invite people to collab-orate toward improving a company.

Take Stock of Your Power
If you are a shareholder for a public company or have access and connec-tions to people with investments in corporations that you want to move on a specific issue, organize! Use the valuable data and information you receive as a stockholder to help inform your strategy and decisions. If you're a valued employee at a company, find out if other valued employees share your activist goal, and present a pos-itive but firm united front. If you have a big social media following, use it to encourage your followers to take action alongside you!

Bring Down the Bullies
Although it may not seem doable, taking down an oppressor (no matter how rich, famous, revered, or buffered by their corporations or management

team) is possible. Courage is contagious, and when everyday revolutionaries speak out and come together in solidarity, our mighty power expands exponentially. If you start to second-guess yourself, remember that no matter how powerful they are, the oppressors we're working to take down answer to someone . . . funders, corporate boards, the Supreme Court, advertisers, and so forth. Michelle Obama famously said, "When they go low, we go high," which is something we should take seriously and literally when speaking truth to power and taking action. Here's our take: "When they go low, we go higher up their org chart—to their overlords or to their shareholders, and apply economic pressure—and then we win!"

Be Seen and Heard
If you're engaging in economic action, keep both your community and your targets (and their advertisers, investors, and other stakeholders) updated on the progress of your campaign through your mission statement, list of demands, updates of how many new people have joined your growing movement, and by copying targets on the petitions and emails you receive from supporters. Economic pressure is best applied in a visible and powerful way to help communicate to your targets that you're here, you're strong, and you will not be moved until transformation happens.

RESOURCE LINKS

Harvard Business Review
"When Do Company Boycotts Work?" https://hbr.org/2012/08/when-do-company-boycotts-work

SocialFunds
"Step-by-Step Guide to Filing a Shareholder Resolution" www.socialfunds.com/sa/resolution.cgi

Proxy Preview
Helping Shareholders Vote Their Values https://www.proxypreview.org

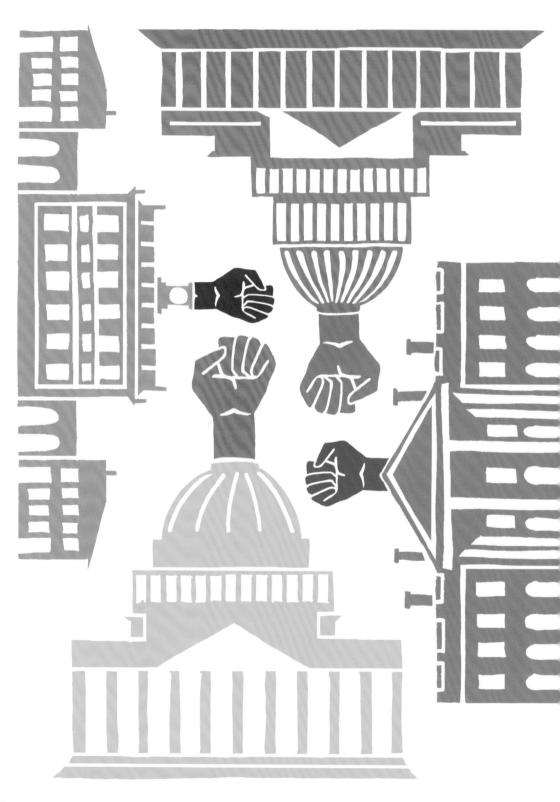

4

GETTING INTO (AND OUT OF) THE GOVERNMENT

he manifestation of American democracy is, at its core, the American government. But how well do you know how things really work in government? We're not talking about arcane parliamentary procedures in the Senate or other mystifying details like that, but big-picture questions:

- What does the federal government do, as opposed to state and local governments?

- What do political parties do, as opposed to the government?

- If you wanted to change a law, regulation, or policy, what would you do?

- How safe is your vote? How much does your vote matter—and when does it matter most?

With civic education in schools on the decline (and most of us not thinking much about the three branches of government once we're out the door of our academic institutions), it's important to remember that we, the people, are supposed to be in control.

We're here to urge you to (and help you) act within the system to change it.

Marching and protesting are only part of an engaged citizen's job. Making an economic vote with your dollars every single day is critical, but your vote in the ballot box is no less so.

Being "the change you want to see in the world" should include considering becoming one of those people making decisions that affect day-to-day life in your city, county, state, and even country.

If you're dissatisfied with the current way government or political parties operate, you can even take more radical steps to try to shake things up at the structural level.

Every decision to implement an inequitable dress code in your child's school is made by people in your school district. Every decision to have local police wear body cameras is made by people in your city. Every decision to create low-income or no-income housing for your local homeless population is made by people in your county. Every decision about drawing and redrawing state and national representation districts is made by people in your state.

People like you. And people who *answer* to you.

In this chapter, we will explore how government and political parties operate at every level so that you can find your place in these systems and determine how to best move the levers of power. There are lots of great resources out there (see the "Takeaways and Resources" section of this chapter, on page 126) about contacting and influencing your government representatives. We will touch on that topic, but we're most interested in you knowing more about becoming one of the people that citizens try to contact and influence.

Look to this chapter to explain the following:

- The typical roles and responsibilities of local versus state versus federal governments

- What political parties do versus what government does, and what local and state parties are responsible for versus the party national committees

- How to get started participating in your local party and local government—regardless of your network or net worth

- The power of (and threats to) your vote and the votes of your fellow citizens

- If you want more radical structural change, the basic roadmap to building a viable third party and reforming the electoral college

Along the way, you'll hear from a variety of ordinary Americans who have run for office, served on commissions, and found ways to participate in democracy in their town, state, and country, most while holding down full-time jobs and more. They did it. None came from a political dynasty. You can do it too.

FIELD NOTES
TERMS AND CONCEPTS TO KNOW

checks and balances: The U.S. federal government has three branches: the executive branch, the judicial branch, and the legislative branch; and those three are meant to be a check on one another's use of power and to share a balance of power between them. See this chapter's U.S. Government org chart (page 96) to get a sense of what each branch does.

civics: The study of the rights and responsibilities of citizenship. Civic education used to be a mandatory subject studied by every American high school student, but it's now an elective in some (usually private) schools' curricula.

direct democracy: The concept that people vote directly on policy initiatives. While citizens across the United States engage in direct democracy for various local and state initiatives, at a national level, the United States is a representative democracy—we vote for representatives; and they vote on our behalf.

electoral college: Another example of representative democracy. Rather than the president of the United States being elected by direct democracy (as in, the total, national popular vote),

the president is elected by the electoral college. Each state assigns "electors" who cast their state's electoral votes for the president. The process of assigning those electors and allocating their votes differs from state to state.

grassroots: Refers to a movement or effort that grows from the bottom up, typically with interested people self-organizing in the beginning, rather than being directed by an elite or leadership group (i.e., top down).

lobbyist: A person who is hired by a special interest group of some kind to try to influence legislators and legislation. While the common perception is that lobbyists always represent special interests that are corporate, lobbyists are hired to represent nonprofits too.

political parties: Private organizations of people who share, at least in theory, the same political philosophy, values, and goals. Those goals are outlined in the party's "platform." In the United States, political parties are neither defined nor required by the Constitution.

primaries: A preliminary election that determines the candidates for the final general election, typically held in November. Primaries are not only held in each state to elect the president every four years, they are also held in most states for many important national, state, and local elected positions. States can have different rules for their primaries, defining which voters can vote for which primary candidates based on their registered political party. State political parties also have the authority to decide to allocate their delegates to a candidate based on a caucus, rather than a traditional primary. Unlike the secret ballot cast during a traditional primary, caucuses are where party members cast their vote in front of one another.

secession: The concept of formally withdrawing from a larger organization or association. The most common usage refers to a state or region separating from a larger nation to become an independent entity. Internationally, secession has happened both peacefully and not so peacefully—for example, the diplomatic split of Czechoslovakia into Slovakia and the Czech Republic, and the very bloody breakup of Yugoslavia. Secession is different from the kind of separation Virginia and West Virginia had, where both stayed in the Union.

swing state: A state that could swing toward either the Democratic or Republican candidate for president, and which therefore gets the lion's share of attention from both parties and media during a campaign.

U.S. Constitution: The founding document establishing the law of the United States. It articulates the rights of the individual, defines how the federal branches of government should work, and delineates states' rights in relation to the federal government. Originally consisting of a preamble and seven articles, it has been amended (through an arduous process) twenty-seven times, with the first ten amendments most commonly referred to as the *Bill of Rights*.

voter suppression: Efforts to deny the vote to eligible citizens. Prior to the Civil Rights movement, legislated voter suppression could manifest in numerous ways, from charging money to vote (i.e., a poll tax) to actual physical intimidation and violence. Voter restriction and suppression actions that still occur today include those passed as state laws (such as voter ID laws) and those enacted by decree (such as targeted reduced polling locations and hours).

Voting Rights Act (VRA): Passed in 1965, a law to ensure that the Fourteenth and Fifteenth Amendment rights to vote for racial minorities were upheld. The VRA includes both general provisions, applicable nationwide, and special provisions, applicable in certain jurisdictions (determined by a "coverage formula") where voter suppression of minorities was rampant. In 2013, the Supreme Court struck down the coverage formula, hence leaving those special provisions effectively unenforceable.

A LOCAL, STATE, AND FEDERAL GOVERNMENT ORG CHART

THE UNITED STATES CONSTITUTION

FEDERAL

Executive Branch	Legislative Branch	Judicial Branch
The president Cabinet and departments Implements law	Senate House of Representatives Writes the laws	Supreme Court Federal courts Rules on constitutionality of laws

Only the feds can:
Print money
Declare war
Make foreign alliance and trade agreements

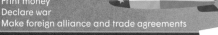

STATE

Executive Branch	Legislative Branch	Judicial Branch
Governor	State senate State legislature or General Assembly	State Supreme Courts Lower state courts

Only a state can:
Set voting process
Assign presidential electors
Draw state and federal legislative districts

LOCAL

County	City	School District

Commissioners or
  board of supervisors
County courts and
  law enforcement
Transportation
Election services
Social services
County clerk and assessor
	Mayor
	City councils
	City manager
	Municipal courts and
	  law enforcement
	Public works, planning,
	  and permits
		School superintendent
		  (professional) and school
		  board (citizens)
		Curricula
		Administrative staffing
		Policies, such as discipline
		  and dress code

WHAT POLITICAL PARTIES DO
VERSUS WHAT GOVERNMENT DOES

Political parties in the United States are private organizations, not government organizations. They are neither defined in nor required by the Constitution. When you join a political party, you're becoming a member of a club, and that club sets its own rules. In many ways, the structure that most parties have developed mirrors the U.S. government structure. This tack is taken with an aim to be successful within that government structure. Specifically, parties have a national organization, but a lot of power and autonomy is granted to state leadership. Despite being private organizations, parties are subject to governmental authority on some issues. It's instructive to know how laws, regulations, and policies at the national level of both government and political parties roll down to the state and local levels, and it's equally helpful to understand the decisions and actions that are left to those distributed levels.

Decentralization is, as in government, an inoculation against tyranny and conspiracy. For example, while the presidential delegate allocation process is decided at the national level, voter registration and primary processes are determined by the state government. Additionally, actual voting is organized and executed at the county level, making it hard to imagine the coordination required to guarantee particular election outcomes. Of course, it can also make it hard to figure out how to approach making change. Whether you want to focus on flipping one of your nearby districts or you want to advocate for changing a platform plank at the national level, understanding where the power to affect those changes lies will make for more efficient use of your time.

The following is a quick primer on what each level of a major political party is responsible for, what it's not responsible for, and how the government at each level has an impact on parties as private organizations.

THE NATIONAL COMMITTEE

- Sets overall national strategy, including messaging and some funding allocation.

- Hosts the national convention, where, among other things, the party's presidential candidate is nominated and accepts the nomination.

- Negotiates and publishes the party platform, which articulates the party's position on political issues of the day.

- Determines overall primary delegate allocation process. At their presidential conventions, both the Democratic and Republican Parties have "unpledged" delegates who are not allocated based on the votes in the states. How a party's unpledged delegates are selected and how they decide how to vote is handled differently by each party.

- Raises money to help party candidates, mostly at the national level. Both parties have national subcommittees that focus on Senate and House seats.

- What they don't do: Decide candidate selection at the local and state levels. Parties don't control much of the rules and processes of how voting gets done (and tabulated) at state and local levels since parties typically opt to take advantage of the election processes and infrastructure that the government provides.

- How the federal government impacts political parties: Sets campaign finance regulation that impacts how all candidates can raise and spend money.

THE STATE PARTY

- Determines the state's election primary process, including whether the state will vote for a presidential candidate via a primary, a caucus, or both.

- Sends leadership to the national committee and national convention to participate in the process of developing the party platform and nominations.

- Often develops its own platform, which may align with, but can also diverge from, the national party platform.

- Issues resolutions on both state-specific and state-government-driven policy, as well as national policy as it pertains to the state.

- Leads fundraising and "get out the vote" (GOTV) efforts, from registration drives to phone banking.

- What they don't do: Unless the state party has a private caucus approach to its presidential primary, it is not always responsible for deciding when election primaries are or how party members can vote in them.

- How the state government impacts political parties: State parties are subject to the same campaign finance rules as the national committee. States can set overall election processes that dictate how party primaries are run. For example, the California electorate recently voted to change their primary election approach to one that sends the top two vote-getters in the primary to the general election to determine the final winner, as opposed to the former process, which mandated that the general election would always be between a Republican and a Democrat. States can also dictate whether their primaries are open or closed, determining whether people can cross party lines for primary elections. Some state parties employ the private caucus approach to their presidential primaries, so that the state party schedules, organizes, and runs the caucuses independently. However, most states integrate their presidential primary process into the state's overall election process so that they are subject to state rules around voting locations, methods, hours, registration, identification requirements, and more.

THE COUNTY COMMITTEE

- Supports and develops local candidates and advocates for local positions and policy initiatives.

- Makes local endorsements of both candidates, as well as on local and state initiatives and propositions.

- Sends leadership to the state party and state convention to participate in the process of developing any state party platforms, endorsements, resolutions, and nominations.

- Fundraising and GOTV efforts, from registration drives to phone banking

- What they don't do: Again, barring the existence of a private presidential primary caucus, local parties don't organize, manage, or tabulate results from elections.

- How the local government impacts political parties: Typically, local governments organize and run election logistics, including the primaries. Volunteers who run local polling places across the country are often recruited and trained at the county level. Some local offices are run as nonpartisan races, according to that locality's charter. Candidates may certainly be forthcoming about their party, but their party is not cited in any election materials.

ERIN VILARDI

FOUNDER OF VOTE RUN LEAD, AN ORGANIZATION DEDICATED TO TRAINING WOMEN TO RUN FOR OFFICE AT ANY LEVEL

Erin Vilardi has trained tens of thousands of women to run for office over the past fifteen years, and she is seeing more women than ever step up and sign up to do so. She shared with us a basic primer on why you—yes, *you*—should think about running for office, and how to start an exploratory committee of one to figure out what to run for and how to do so.

Why Run Now?

"Prior to the November 2016 election, two-thirds of women in our program were interested in developing a five-year plan for running for office, and VoteRunLead would try to convince them to run sooner. Since that election, more women are saying, 'Okay. I'll run for office, and I want to run *now*.'

"Prior to the November 2016 election, women ran for office because they cared about specific issues, and often they ran only after they'd been asked to. Since that election, more women have realized that government is where a lot of power lies, and that it is having a disproportionate impact on their daily lives. And they are not represented.

"Women today are pissed off—about so many issues. And they want to save democracy. A lot of women woke up on November 9 and realized there was a big gap between where they thought the country was and where it really was.

"There's been a shift, and women are saying to themselves, 'If Trump can be president, I can surely run for city council.'"

Time + Money = The Winning Equation

"There's no getting around it. The higher the office, the more money matters. So, for example, both men and women enter politics and build from there.

Bottom line:

- Local races can cost up to $10,000.
- State races can start at around $25,000 and range up to $250,000 for a big state.
- Federal office (i.e., the House or Senate) will cost millions of dollars.

"The good news is that being someone who is *not* rich, privileged, or connected can be an asset in today's political climate. But if you don't start with money, get ready to spend more time. Start preparing earlier. Start fundraising earlier. Start

---

Erin and VoteRunLead launched the Run As You Are campaign in early 2017, which has, so far, trained eight thousand women to run for office.

getting involved with local political people and events ASAP. And knock on twice as many doors.

"Plan on longer lead times and more engagement with people—as potential donors, volunteers, and just people who will know you, recognize you, and endorse you—to balance a lack of starting capital."

Seize the Day—and the Office

"Identifying what office to run for boils down to three questions:

- Where do you live? You run where you live. Get to know your district, city, county, state offices and commissions, and who represents you now.
- What are the top three things you care about? Ask yourself this and find out what legislative body works on those issues. When you figure out where those issues are being worked on, get a face-to-face meeting with local politicians who seem to care about the issues and are actively discussing them. They will tell you how it all works together (city, county, state, federal). Don't worry if you're just learning about all the committees and commissions and other opportunities in your area. Political information has value and leads to power, so it is not always shared freely. Plus, government is catching up on using technology to spread the word, so it's no surprise you may not know the inner workings of government in your area.
- Assess your own leadership, activities, relationships to community, and so on. Who are you, and would you vote for yourself? Imposter syndrome is real. Men and women have it. So does Beyoncé.

Know that it's there—you can't shake it. Acknowledge it. I call it 'crazy Erin.' But I don't let it stop me."

Human Networking Is Number One in the Political Space

"Reach out and have conversations with people who have done what you want to do. This is one case where conversations are more efficient than online searching.

"Go out and start attending local and community meetings. Get to learn what the various local offices do. How often do they meet? How much time does it take to participate?

"Remember: You do not have to know everything to get into politics. There are people hired to craft and write bills for you, for example. Even city councils have clerks. You are supposed to learn on the job. Being a lifelong learner is the kind of attitude that's needed.

"Politics is an IRL (in real life) sport. You have to show up."

This Democracy Can Be Saved

"I'm optimistic because this is more than a political moment. It's a cultural moment around what kind of America and Americans we want to be. What kind of leaders do we want? We've been neglecting government, but I'm optimistic because we're going to see a new generation of political entrepreneurs. We need that spirit and energy."

ELECTION KNOW-HOW

David Cohen was on an appointed library commission and is now an elected school board member and Democratic Party County Committee official. Sanjay Dave is an elected school board member. Megan Hunt is a longtime community activist running for the Nebraska state legislature. Courtney Macavinta serves as an appointee on the Santa Clara County Juvenile Justice Commission. Erica Mauter serves on her city's Capital Long-Range Improvement Committee and ran for city council. Keith Stattenfield was a library commission appointee and then a planning commission appointee.

When you talk to people who have sought and achieved local office, common themes emerge. Echoing the advice of Erin Vilardi, these local officials emphasize the value of showing up, connecting with people in real life, and figuring out where your passions and skills match the job description.

WHAT'S MY MOTIVATION?

David Cohen always had a general sense of civic duty and wanted to serve. But for other folks, it's more specific, as in the case of school board member Sanjay Dave, who had kids in school, became fascinated by the topic of education and how to help all children learn better, and saw school board participation as a way to institute policies that would help. Courtney Macavinta leads a nonprofit addressing the school-to-prison pipeline, so she was specifically interested in the juvenile justice commission because of its relevance to that work.

Keith Stattenfield had yet another motivation: He first became interested in the city's planning commission when a huge development was proposed near his house. He attended meetings and realized what the commission did was a good match for his skills, so he eventually applied, got appointed, and served for eight years. Then there's Erica Mauter, who knew that filling both elected and appointed roles at the local level was part of the Republican Party's pipeline-filling strategy, so she sought a similar role in a potential Democratic Party pipeline. Megan Hunt is equally aware of the pipeline, having fought from the

Similarly, David researched all the local commissions, found out which ones had openings, and learned about the process for applying: "I picked the two commissions that were most interesting to me and applied for both with the hope of being appointed to one. I ended up getting an appointment to the library commission. Once I started to serve, I determined that I wanted to move to elected office, preferably city council, in the future. So I set up a meeting with a mentor who was serving on the San Jose City Council, to learn what steps I should take and what résumé I should build to eventually achieve my goal."

For Courtney, it was important for her to know what the commission did; she wanted a "working commission." Erica got her start with volunteer work, both on local boards and on local campaigns. Ultimately, she worked hard on the campaign of her city's current mayor, and it was the mayor who invited her to join the city committee. Once she decided to run for city council, she reached out to people she knew who had been involved in local campaigns and politics and asked for advice. As she put it, "Every elected official I know has their 'kitchen cabinet,' and I formed mine."

HOW MUCH DOES IT COST (IN TIME AND MONEY)?

Being appointed to commissions is obviously "cheap" in terms of money, with no campaign to mount, but it does take time. For example, Keith's planning commission role required three to ten hours of meetings a month, all at night, plus a few hours before each meeting to read materials and research. Courtney spends ten to twelve hours a month on the juvenile justice commission, including site visits to local facilities. David admits his family has at times been concerned about the amount of hours he spends in his civic roles.

Running for office (even a local office in a smaller city) has costs. Sanjay's first (unsuccessful) run for school board is a good case study: "My first campaign, I just threw myself in and learned as I went. I knew squat. I didn't even know it cost money, let alone $2,400, to register. I had to learn how to write a campaign statement, what papers I had to file, how much funding I needed. Needless to say, I stumbled through it, got a lot of advice from many people, and learned a lot. Most of the administrative resources were from the local government website and county electoral office. I made many calls to them to understand timelines and forms. I consulted with other elected officials on campaign tactics—how to design a website, mailers, flyers, and who to get endorsements from, and so on. Campaign costs can vary quite a bit, depending on the number of competitors you have and how well known you already are. My first time around I spent over $10,000, but this last time, I spent only $1,200 for lawn signs. I ended up running unopposed, but I had already decided I was going to spend a lot less and focus on getting my name out early and getting the key endorsements needed from other community leaders that people trust." Megan hasn't been quite as lucky in her current run for state legislature, and there's more to running for office than you may realize at first. "In our most recent election cycle, the candidates in my legislative district ran the most expensive race in the history of the Nebraska legislature, with over half a million dollars raised by their campaigns. I spend about forty hours a week on my campaign with fundraising, phone calls, talking to press, events, and knocking on doors in my district. I am also still running my company forty hours a week. The commitment and focus, and the mental and emotional stamina it takes to run for office, is significant. It is absolutely not something to take lightly."

David agrees: "Running for office can be complicated. Having to balance fundraising, meeting people, walking precincts, coordinating volunteers, and planning/distributing campaign literature takes experience and time. It is good to have help from somebody who has been involved in a campaign before. During the two months before the election, the campaign can take up almost all free time. It is often necessary to take time off from work to get things done. Each of my campaigns has cost about $10,000. I was able to fundraise about 80 percent of the money I needed each time I ran. To be a successful fundraiser, get over the discomfort of asking for money. You have to be willing to ask everyone. The worst that can happen is they say no."

Erica is granular about what she thinks it will take her to run for city council in her "big little city": "It will be in the $30–35,000 range, paying for staff people, literature and lawn signs, printing costs, and things like designing and maintaining the website and online tools. It didn't take a lot of work to raise $20,000, given the size of my ward. As for time, I knock on doors three to four days a week. If I have a free hour in the evening, I go do two blocks. I'd estimate I'm spending twenty hours a week for the campaign, on top of working my full-time day job."

> **Key Points**
>
> The Time + Money equation holds true. The more money you start out with, the less time you'll have to spend campaigning, fundraising, and coalition-building.

Most of the local officials and appointees we spoke to did not succeed their first time around, but they examined the reasons and went back for a second try with a better sense of what was required. Many people make their first attempt, and if they don't win or aren't selected, they stop. Each of the local officials we spoke to kept going. They kept attending meetings; they kept meeting and building relationships with people.

Sanjay puts it bluntly: "What I learned my first go-around was that local campaigns are a popularity contest, like high school. People vote for their friends or who they know best, not necessarily the best candidate. I learned you need to start early and you need to have people know your name and have good thoughts about you."

Once you achieve your goal and get elected or appointed, you may find yourself disappointed too—in people. As David put it: "It is inevitable that as an appointed or elected official, you will find yourself in the middle of a dispute. It is never pleasant to experience in person. There can be real anger and damaged relationships that run deep. It is how one navigates these conflicts that deter-mines how successful one is as a public servant. You have to have a thick skin to be able to work as part of the team." Megan adds that you have to get through conflicts with people: "What I have learned is that you're not going to agree with everyone all of the time, and you have to have a bit of amnesia with politics because you never know who you are going to have to work with. There are folks we never think we'll have common ground with, but we find a shared goal and end up needing each other."

Erica, having seen firsthand how much is hap-pening at the local level, has been disappointed in low voter turnout, especially in local-only elections. Finally, Courtney issued a reminder that when it comes to appointed commissions, they often make recommendations, not mandates.

> **Key Points**
>
> If at first you don't succeed, try, try again. And remember that people are people—the good, the bad, and the indif-ferent—in politics, as in life.

CAN YOU MAKE IT IF YOU'RE NOT RICH OR CONNECTED?

Remember: Time + Money in some combination is the answer. If you have a big idea and want to start a business, but you don't have a ton of money, then it's a good idea to start saving money to launch it. The same goes for wanting to run a campaign. Start now building your resources—not only financial resources but also the relationships that will lead you to resources. Check with your city or county and see if they subsidize the registration costs for low-income candidates. If money is a significant concern, keep in mind that serving on commissions can be a path to running for office, though it doesn't have to be. Either way, it can be very productive for building your network. Check out your city or county site and find out the opportunities—some commissions even have "youth commissions," as the juvenile justice commission Courtney serves on does, so that you can participate even as a teenager.

Is it important for those of us outside the rich, connected (and often white) demographics to go for these roles? According to Sanjay, "You will notice that most public offices are made up of white men and then white women. We need more diversity in our public officials because there is just too much unconscious bias. I want to encourage more people of color and women to run for public office. If you don't have the means yourself, ask for donations early and seek advice from a current or former official on effective fundraising."

Erica takes that to heart, saying, "The extent that my being present and visible plants the seed with someone else that they can do it—that's important." And Megan believes in as much seed planting as possible: "Lack of perseverance, ambition, or drive isn't to blame for the deficit of diversity in our community leadership across lines of gender, class, and race. It's the systemic inequality, something white women honestly cannot experience to the same degree as those with other aspects of difference and identity. To see progress, forward-thinking change, and compassion across the fabric of our community, we have to acknowledge that looking to our left and right—at our own peers—isn't the way to build the relationships that will lead to our collective or individual growth, in politics or otherwise. To serve people, leaders must consciously unlearn their beliefs and thought patterns that reinforce sexism, heteronormativity, classism, and whiteness."

David has additional tactical advice: "Politics is about relationships. It is helpful to put in the time as a volunteer and get to know the people who can be helpful in running for office. Seek out a mentor to help navigate the system and introduce you to people. The more connections you have, the more help you will get. Help can take the form of volunteer time or financial donations. Reach out to people outside of your immediate circle. Find a primary supporter from each constituency group to advocate for you in that group and help you meet people."

And Erica adds, "For me, it was a long series of someone who is doing something asking me to support them, and I said 'Okay.' It was relationship building. Showing up for stuff—council meetings, public hearings, et cetera. You meet people, and you learn stuff. Who else is sitting at that meeting? If you have strong neighborhood associations, show up to those. If you're already volunteering somewhere else—church, a nonprofit organization, et cetera—you can take help from other people there who don't live in your district. They can donate; they can volunteer."

MAKING AN IMPACT: IS IT REAL?

If it's true, as Keith states, that "at a very local level, city council is not terribly well paid, spends a lot of time working, and generally doesn't get much credit or thanks for their efforts," why sign up for that? Because you can indeed have a very real impact—and positively affect real people in your own community.

- Serve on the library foundation and hear stories about adults finally learning to read thanks to library programs.

- Serve on the planning commission and be the voice of your neighbors in the face of outside developers driven more by profit than by people.

- Serve on a school board and work to improve educational options and school facilities to help children from all walks of life achieve success.

- Serve on the juvenile justice commission and change the age of transfer from juvenile hall to adult prison from eighteen to twenty.

- Serve in any capacity and be able to help an angry or disenfranchised community member find a solution to their problem.

- Serve on your chosen political party's county committee and help get people who share your values elected.

Key Points

The impact is real. It's why we wrote this book.

WHAT IF YOU'RE NOT AN EXTROVERT?

Okay, #RealTalk: All this "talk to people" advice can be daunting if you're not an extrovert. Make sure your search for ways to participate includes appointed commission and committee work that might be more up your alley than running for office. You still need to interact with people, but perhaps not on such a large scale. You can get to know a smaller number of people more deeply, something at which introverts often excel.

Key Points

Plenty of elected and appointed officials do not identify as extroverts. It's not a prerequisite to serve. So heed Megan's advice: "Never sell yourself short— you are good enough. Show the world why you matter; don't wait for it to ask you. Be very, very brave."

HOW TO EMBED YOURSELF IN YOUR LOCAL POLITICAL PARTY

Another way to affect local issues is to get more involved with your political party of choice. Political party activities have tremendous influence on local government. Often, local party leadership cultivates candidates for office because people aren't lining up for all positions. Parties make endorsements on local candidates and ballot initiatives, and many members follow those recommendations without much question. If your party is the majority party, you can still help steer where the party lands on the left-to-right spectrum. If your party is the minority party, you can help flip your state!

Most local party machines are not impossible to penetrate. They're more likely to be desperate for local involvement and engagement.

The first step is showing up. The second step is offering to pitch in. The third step is pulling aside someone doing something you find interesting and asking them how they got involved. At the county level, there are few political dynasties; there's mostly just a few neighbors taking the time to be there.

FACT FINDING: DRILL DOWN TO THE COUNTY LEVEL

Look for the following information:

- County committee officers and their contact info
- The schedule for monthly county committee meetings (Hint: Start going!)
- Links to local issues and candidates
- Volunteering needs, like phone banking and door knocking

Find Your Local Party

Here's how to find out where to go and what to do.

Start at your party's national site

Democrats: https://www.democrats.org

Republicans: https://www.gop.com

Third parties too: we'll use the Green Party as an example—www.gp.org

Each National site has a link to the party's web presence in the 50 states

Democrats: https://asdc.democrats.org/state-parties

Republicans: https://www.gop.com/leaders/states

The Green Party: www.gp.org/state_parties

Most state sites have a single link where you can find all counties listed; here are some examples

aldemocrats.org/local/all

nebraskademocrat**s.org/get-local**

www.wisdems.or**g/county-parties**

https://www.cagop.org/counties

https://www.nygop.org/county-chairs

www.mngoplocalparties.com

https://www.cagreens.org/county-parties

https://gpfl.org/affiliates

MAKING A THIRD PARTY VIABLE

The Constitution was written before our current political parties existed. But modern-day efforts to elect third-party candidates to the presidency have failed due to the political economics of campaign financing, over a century of mostly bipartisan political patterning, and the grassroots organizing needed to convince voters that a new party could win and thrive.

Nonetheless, in one of the most controversial and divisive election cycles in U.S. history, 2016 voters turned out for third-party candidates in significant numbers. Although they weren't conclusively a deciding factor, they made a small but substantial impact on the outcome in key battleground states.

The last time third-party voters turned out in numbers that significantly contributed to shaping an election result was when an Independent, Ross Perot, garnered 19 percent of the vote in 1992. There was also controversy in 2000 over the role that Green Party candidate Ralph Nader played, especially in the deciding state of Florida. The growing momentum behind third-party movements and the level of enthusiasm Independent senator–turned–Democratic presidential primary candidate–turned–Independent senator Bernie Sanders amassed raises the question, *What would it take to create a viable third party?*

START LOCALLY

Increase visibility and shift negative perceptions about the role and impact of third parties on close presidential races by running local candidates for state legislature, city council, school board, and mayoral positions. Once third parties have a robust network at the local level, their credibility, recognition, and ability to fundraise and organize for higher office increases.

DO YOUR HOMEWORK

There's a lot of paperwork to become a viable candidate. Make sure you read and understand all of the bureaucratic processes before jumping in unprepared. If possible, find out how many petition signatures you need to collect and by what deadline before you announce your candidacy so that you can plan your strategy and financial approach. Refer to the Federal Election Commission (FEC), your state board of elections, and the U.S. Election Assistance Commission.

MONEY MATTERS

Ensure that you understand campaign finance rules, and research whether or not you're required to fund your campaign. For presidential contests, campaign finance guidelines oblige your party to have obtained a specific number of votes. Make sure that you understand the financial commitment needed for bringing party idea into fruition. If you don't have the resources, take time to build your team of volunteers and focus on fundraising.

Study what independent voters in your community care about. Engage in focus groups, analyze data and surveys, canvass and phone bank to know your constituents.

RUN ON A DIVERSE AND INCLUSIVE PLATFORM

Show that your party is interested in actualizing change at all levels, not just on garnering support for a particular issue.

MOBILIZE THE NEXT GENERATION

Invest in training, organizing, recruiting, and mentoring young leaders to work their way up from smaller local positions to statewide and potentially national policy-making roles.

WHAT WOULD IT TAKE TO REFORM THE ELECTORAL COLLEGE?

When we complain about the system that our federal government has settled into, two significant complaints focus on (a) the previously discussed two-party system (which is not defined in the Constitution), and (b) the method of determining our president through the electoral college (which is defined). Article 2 of the Constitution affirms that each state shall have the same number of electors as congressional representatives and senators, but that the electors cannot be senators or representatives. Furthermore, it gives states complete leeway in determining how to assign their electors, with later Supreme Court cases allowing only minor oversight from the federal government to ensure electors aren't assigned via a corrupt process.

The electoral college was considered a compromise, even as it was ratified, between those who wanted more of a direct democratic vote for president and those who proposed that Congress (as representatives of their states) determine the president. However, when the Constitution and the electoral college were cooked up, the two-party system had not yet become the norm. There was more concern about a highly fragmented vote, and the logistics of direct democracy were, if nothing else, more time-consuming. The final agreed-upon process was that each state would get the number of electoral votes equal to the total of their number of representatives in the House, plus two more to reflect their senators. The Constitution also guaranteed that every state would be allocated at least one representative (and therefore one electoral vote) in addition to their two senators.

Despite the leeway given to states on how to assign electors, all but two states now have a winner-takes-all approach to assigning their electoral votes. That method wasn't mentioned in the Constitution, and it wasn't initially common, but was adopted by more and more states over time. In the context of today's dominating two-party system, the winner-takes-all approach has led to several common complaints about the electoral college, namely:

- The majority of states are considered relatively safe for one party's nominee or the other, leading to the existence of typically no more than a dozen "swing states" getting the bulk of the attention and thus investment from major political parties. Presidential candidates barely bother to campaign in all fifty states anymore. This lack of presence not only makes voters in those states feel unimportant, it also brings less attention to state and local races in those states.

- The number of representatives in Congress (and therefore the number of electors) has been frozen since 1929. While the allocation of that number among states can be reapportioned after every census, given that the smallest states are entitled to a minimum number of three representatives, there is no way for larger states to have a proportionally accurate number of representatives compared to smaller states.

- Due, in part, to that lack of proportionality, twice in the past five presidential elections the winner of the popular vote did not win the electoral college, and therefore did not become president.

Can the electoral college be improved? Evolved? Abolished altogether? Technically, the only mechanism to abolish the electoral college altogether (or to change how it works across the board nationally) is a constitutional amendment.

There are options that would change how the electoral college works in practice, though. These changes could be enacted at the state level, rather than by constitutional amendment. If enough states sign on, there's your reform. If this is an area where you have interest and passion, here are a few significant electoral reform approaches to consider (and perhaps evangelize).

THE NATIONAL POPULAR VOTE INTERSTATE COMPACT (NPVIC)

The National Popular Vote Interstate Compact is an agreement that states can sign to allocate their electors to the candidate who wins the popular vote nationally. The agreement qualifies that each state's vow to do so only kicks in once states representing more than half of the electoral college votes (i.e., more than the number required to win the presidency) are on board. As of this writing, ten states plus the District of Columbia are signed on, representing 165 electoral votes, or 30.7 percent of the total electoral college, and 61.1 percent of the votes needed to make the concept fly.

This approach creates a simple outcome that the winner of the national popular vote would always be elected president, all without amending the Constitution or officially abolishing the electoral college. The NPVIC approach would mean that every vote in every state would count, eliminating the concept of swing states and encouraging candidates to broaden their campaign strategies. Check out the status of the compact in your state here: https://www.nationalpopularvote.com/state-status

RANKED-CHOICE VOTING (RCV)

Ranked-choice voting allows voters to rank candidates for an office. When votes are tallied, if no candidate wins the majority, the candidate with the lowest number of first-place votes is eliminated, and the second choice-votes of those voters are redistributed to the remaining candidates. This process repeats until one candidate has the clear majority. Some municipalities have already implemented ranked-choice voting for their local races, including San Francisco. The RCV approach helps eliminate the concept of "strategic" voting and the perspective that voting for a third-party candidate is the same as "wasting" a vote. RCV, particularly if it is adopted in more city, county, and state elections, might help build third parties from the ground up, rather than having third parties mostly described as potential spoilers every four years.

PROPORTIONAL ELECTORAL VOTE ALLOCATION

Another method allocates a state's electoral votes based on the popular vote, rather than winner-takes-all. Maine and New Hampshire take an approach that is a step down this path, allocating electoral votes per congressional district, with their two additional electoral votes (representing their two senators) going to the winner of the state's popular vote. Colorado considered unilaterally switching to a proportional allocation of their electoral votes in the last decade but ultimately rejected it. Unlike taking part in the NPVIC, a state going it alone with proportional electoral vote allocation would likely dilute their impact on the race, and therefore their importance to the candidates. Interestingly, the two main political parties have different primary delegate allocation processes. The Democratic National Committee (DNC) allocates delegates proportionally by state, based on the popular vote, with a caveat that a candidate must get at minimum 15 percent of a state's popular vote to get any delegates at all. The Republican National Committee (RNC) allocation process used to be winner-takes-all, and most states still follow this process, but some states have started to shift to proportional allocation. In 2016, for example, when the Republicans ran a large number of candidates early, the winner-takes-all approach solidified President Trump's lead in a more lopsided fashion than his aggregate popular vote in the primaries would have.

The nation's founders purposely made it challenging to enact sweeping reform at the federal level. Each of the preceding approaches is an example of tackling electoral college reform at the state level instead. Start by asking your state legislators their position on reforming your state's allocations of electoral votes.

HOW TO PROTECT YOUR, AND OTHER PEOPLE'S, VOTE

Elections are your chance to change your country and the conversation. The 2016 presidential election highlighted existing concerns about gerrymandering, money in politics, and voter suppression and restriction in the form of everything from new voter ID laws to reduced polling locations and hours in low-opportunity neighborhoods. So it's no wonder that some Americans ask themselves, "Why bother voting at all?" Voting is about far more than presidential elections (although those come with the additional ramifications of the opportunity to make lifetime Supreme Court appointments). We also vote for members of Congress, state legislatures, local councils, school boards, and even for some judicial and law enforcement roles. This guide will help you be a more cautious and prepared voter, to safeguard your vote in advance, and alert you to risks.

BEFORE ELECTION DAY

Register now. Register well in advance of the election—before sites start crawling and staffers become zombies. Double-check that you're legitimately in the system, and get proof of registration with a screen capture or paper trail. Find your registration deadline on WorkingAmericaVotes.org /register or https://www.vote411.org.

Your name here. Ensure that the name on your birth certificate and the name on your voter registration are the same. Even a misplaced accent mark could prevent you from voting.

Avoid polling-place panic. Ever gone to your polling place and found it vacant? Polling areas can be moved between elections. Even though the printed voter guide you receive by mail should include your polling-place address, type your home address into this nifty polling-place locator every time to be sure you know your poll location: https://www.vote411.org.

Know the where and the when. Restricted polling hours can affect when and if you can vote. Avoid this pitfall. Figure out when it's most likely to be crowded: Before and after traditional working hours, lines can get long and tiresome, and you may give up hope, so bring comfortable shoes— and snacks!

Absentee ballots. Out of town on Election Day? Make sure you research your state's laws regarding your ballot in advance. Every state is different. Consider becoming a permanent absentee voter if your state allows it, especially if you're a frequent traveler or homebound.

Fight disinformation. Are you sure that the mailer you received has correct voting information and is from your county registrar of voters or from the party with which you're registered? Certain special interest groups have been caught sending out misleading endorsement information or even absentee-ballot/voting instructions that looked legitimate but weren't. Even if such tactics are uncovered pre–Election Day, the damage is already done.

ON ELECTION DAY

Bring your license and registration. Even if your state doesn't require it, bring your identification and proof of registration anyway.

Your Voting Checklist
(Courtesy of the League of Women Voters)

Make sure you know:

- Registration deadlines
- Voter qualifications and registration forms
- Election dates
- Early voting and absentee-ballot options
- Ballot measure and candidate information for federal, state, and local races
- Polling place locations, hours, and ID requirements
- Voting machine instructions

Disability ability. The Voting Accessibility for the Elderly and Handicapped Act ensures that you can bring a non-employer or non-officer of your union to assist you in the act of voting if you're disabled or cannot speak English.

THE DIFFERENCE BETWEEN DIRECT LOBBYING AND GRASSROOTS LOBBYING

Grassroots lobbying in support of an issue or a cause is commonly referred to as advocacy. Direct lobbying is lobbying with the goal of influencing, supporting, proposing, adopting, or rejecting a particular piece of legislation.

Since each type of lobbying comes with different rules and regulations from the IRS, it's important that you are in compliance with tax law. How these laws impact you will depend on whether you are working with a 501(c)(3) nonprofit, a business, or a private foundation. Visit your state attorney general's website for more information about each of these tax statuses and how they are regulated in your neck of the woods.

FOCUS ON THE LOCAL

Visit https://www.usa.gov for help identifying who represents you and how to contact them. Research whom to lobby by identifying your local legislators online. You can do this and learn more about how grassroots lobbying is regulated in your state by reading your state board of elections site. Ensure that you're reaching out to the right person who has the power to help give you what you want. Finally, many officials ask for your zip code to determine whether or not you're a constituent. Be proactive by answering that question up front when setting up meetings or making calls.

ORGANIZE YOUR PEOPLE

Whether you're planning a lobby day with in-person meetings, holding a call-in drive, or delivering petitions, there's power in numbers. These people translate into voters in the eyes of the staff and the politicians themselves.

PICK THE STRATEGIC APPROACH

Capitol Hill (Washington, DC) and local district office staff repeatedly express that social media callouts are less impactful than phone calls and in-person lobbying meetings. While emails, letters, and faxes (yes, they still accept faxes!) are important because they are usually tallied by subject matter and theme, face-to-face meetings and phone calls put a human face and voice on the issues.

SET UP A MEETING

If you want to meet while in Washington, DC, dial the U.S. Capitol switchboard to arrange a meeting with your elected official. If you want to meet with your representative at home, dial their local office. You will likely meet with relevant legislative staff members on their team to discuss your concerns or political agenda. Bring in one-page reports, background information on your issue, and contact information that makes it easy for elected officials to follow up if more information is needed.

DELIVER YOUR MESSAGE WITH THE THREE C'S

Be prepared to provide *clear, concise,* and *compelling* commentary on the issues that impact your community. It's good to have your message prepared in advance. Make sure the messaging you use on social media, in petitions, in videos, over the phone, and in your talking points maintains a consistent and reliable narrative.

EMPHASIZE SHARED VALUES AND GOALS

Whether your representative is a friend or foe to the issues you care about, begin your conversation by establishing common ground and stating your mutual interest and commitment to the well-being of your community.

HELP THEM HELP YOU

Elected officials and their staffers are busy and want to know your bottom line. Don't bury the lede. Offer proactive ways that they can provide solutions.

TAKEAWAYS AND RESOURCES

Figure out how things work and use these tips to get involved every day, not every four years.

Politics: Not Just for the Elite!
With all eyes on Washington, it's easy to assume everything important happens there. It's not true. So much you care about, so much you are upset about, so much you are passionate about ... it happens right where you are. Take it from us: Local political parties and local governments are *desperate* for more participation from their citizens. Show up and you can step up and make a real difference.

Time + Money = The Winning Formula
If you want to run for office, big or small, keep the above formula in mind. The less you have of one, the more you need of the other. When it comes to money, ask early and often. When it comes to time, consider it an investment. The formula changes as you expand your network, and get more experience in the political system, but it still boils down to that.

Change Is Hard. Constitutional Change Is Even Harder
The founders made amending the U.S. Constitution a challenging road. They erred on the side of incremental change,

and from the states up and not the other way around. That isn't always the quickest way to change. But being part of that drive for change rather than waiting for it to be decreed from above is why you've made it this far, right?

Strength in Numbers
From the start, we've emphasized getting active in your local community, and we've evangelized the opportunities that the internet and social media present for spreading the word and growing your community of like-minded advocates. Whether you're trying to update your school district's curricula or lobbying your state officials to change how your state assigns its electors, showing you have people standing beside you makes more of an impact. Go to meetings, go door-to-door, go online. Find those people.

It May Not Work How You Think It Works
If you aren't sure how something works, then how can you help encourage the reforms you want? Yes, it may feel like going back to civics class (or taking it for the first time, sadly) but understanding how the vegan sausage is made is step one to mixing metaphors and building a better mousetrap!

RESOURCE LINKS

The text of the Constitution
https://www.archives.gov/
founding-docs/constitution-transcript

United States naturalization civics test study materials
https://www.uscis.gov/citizenship/
learners/study-test/study-materials-
civics-test

Find your elected officials
https://www.usa.gov/elected-officials

Call elected officials with the U.S. Capitol switchboard
202-224-3121

Indivisible's Guide to Influencing Congress
https://www.indivisible.org/guide

Federal Election Commission
https://www.fec.gov

U.S. Election Assistance Commission
https://www.eac.gov

Wikipedia entry on electoral reform efforts (state-by-state links at end)
https://en.wikipedia.org/wiki/
Electoral_reform_in_the_United_States

National Popular Vote site
https://www.nationalpopularvote.com

FairVote on ranked-choice voting
www.fairvote.org/rcv#rcvbenefits

The DNC site
https://www.democrats.org

The RNC site
https://www.gop.com

VoteRunLead
https://voterunlead.org

Emerge America
https://www.emergeamerica.org

Emily's List
https://emilyslist.org

Run for Something
https://www.runforsomething.net

League of Women Voters election information site
https://www.vote411.org

The Election Protection coalition site with state-by-state voting rights information
https://www.866ourvote.org/state

Federal voting rights statutes
https://www.justice.gov/crt/
statutes-enforced-voting-section

REFORM SCHOOL

REFORMING OTHER
INSTITUTIONS IN OUR LIVES

rom the Revolutionary War to teenagers taking on the NRA, the spirit of righteous resistance is ingrained in America's DNA. Dissent is patriotic, and speaking truth to power is as American as apple pie. We've devoted this chapter to exploring how to reform or revolutionize systems and institutions—beyond the government.

Throughout history, visionary rebels with a cause (or two, or three, or many!) have flexed their rights to publicly assemble and practice free speech to fight for a brighter future for the next generation. Those not afforded access to those liberties because of systemic injustice recognized their own dignity, organized their communities and allies, and demanded equal representation.

Discover how to transform public debate and reform the institutions that matter.

In the pages ahead, you'll discover how to do the following:

- Become a savvier media consumer, and perhaps media producer
- Start and sustain your own advocacy group
- Push back on inequitable policies in schools, from biased dress codes to inadequate campus sexual assault policies
- Understand and protect your right to speak, including on campus
- Fight for better health-care access, whether fighting for reproductive rights, acceptable levels of care if trans, or the mandated services and support guaranteed people with disabilities

We're sharing valuable advice from media masters who've used their platforms online, community rabble-rousers building support for a cause and making things happen, and everyday resisters bringing change to the classroom and campus. They all know what it's like to turn a ripple into a tsunami.

We hope the insights gained from everyday revolutionaries will inspire you to lead, because the world needs the strengths only you can offer. Let's go!

FIELD NOTES
TERMS AND CONCEPTS TO KNOW

The Affordable Care Act (ACA):
Also known as "Obamacare," the comprehensive health-care-reform law enacted in March 2010 to make health insurance accessible to more Americans.

gender nonconforming (GNC), genderqueer, or non-binary (NB):
Any gender that does not fit into the constructed male and female binary.

LGBTQIA: A term that includes and makes visible lesbian, gay, bisexual, transgender, intersex, and asexual people within the queer community.

National Endowment for the Arts (NEA): The independent federal agency providing funding and support for Americans to participate in the arts, and explore creativity. The NEA supports art education through partnerships with state arts agencies, local leaders, federal agencies, and the philanthropic sector. Its purpose is to support learning, celebrate America's diverse cultural heritage, and to promote equal access to the arts. Visit https://www.arts.gov.

National Endowment for the Humanities (NEH): The independent federal agency that offers grants to support research, education, and public programs in the humanities. Visit https://www.neh.gov.

safe spaces: Since 1970, many colleges have created areas designated to be free from harassment, bias, threatening actions, or oppressive conversations. Safe spaces have been the focus of debate. Supporters believe that they allow marginalized people, who would otherwise be systemically silenced, to speak. Opponents view them as a threat to the First Amendment.

Title VII: The Civil Rights Act of 1964, outlawing hiring or employment discrimination on the basis of the employee's "race, color, religion, sex, or national origin." Title VII does not cite sexual orientation or gender identity.

Title IX: Law prohibiting sex-based exclusion from or discrimination within educational programs and activities funded by the federal government, providing women with equal access to all services at educational institutions.

trans broken arm syndrome: When doctors claim to not know how to treat routine medical issues among trans people because of misconceptions about their bodies and transphobia. The free press guaranteed

REFORMING THE MEDIA

by the Constitution is a necessary check and watchdog on our government, but we should watch the watchdogs and become ever more savvy media consumers.

HOW TO VET A MEDIA SOURCE

The beauty of the internet is that you now have access to a diverse set of opinions and can see how the rest of the world reports on the same stories. The dark side of the internet is its information overload—and the increasing impact of false information propagated online. In this section, John Boitnott, journalist for such outlets as *Inc.* magazine, *Entrepreneur*, NBC, Business Insider, *USA Today*, *Fortune,* and VentureBeat, shares tips on how to build your media literacy skills and the top six dead giveaways that a news item is false.

DEVELOPING YOUR OWN MEDIA LITERACY SKILLS

Does it push your buttons? The key here is emotionality. Does the article tell a story that makes you tremendously angry or overjoyed? Does it push your buttons—good or bad—in some way? If so, that should put you on guard.

Does the publication have a newsroom? Is it one with reputable journalists paid to research and report on stories? Or is it a website run by a few people mostly making up incendiary headlines? Research the people—and their bona fides—who sit on the mastheads and editorial staffs for the publications you read.

Are they attributing to real sources? Are they sourcing their stories (finding the attributable source of the fact)? If they aren't, leave the site and never come back.

Top Six Giveaways That It's Fake News

Fake then, fake now. Does the site have a history of releasing fake news?

Who's covering what? Are other known reputable news sites covering this story?

Poor writing quality. Are there lots of spelling and grammar mistakes? Are the stories too conversational in tone? If so, a con artist may be writing swill to get you riled up emotionally through lies and manipulation.

A weird domain name is a red flag. Here's an example: houstonchronicle-tv.com. You will also often see "com.co" domains posing as news sites.

Confusing opinion with fact. Statements like "the consensus is" and "most people believe" (with no accompanying polling data) have no place in a news article.

The story is one-sided. Outlets should always try to cover several points of view around an issue (if there *are* several points of view). They should offer each relevant party a chance to comment or respond to allegations. If one side refuses to participate, the news outlet should mention that it at least attempted to get a statement.

Learn the history of journalism. That includes why it exists and what role it plays in modern life. If you don't respect journalists, you're more vulnerable to fake news because you don't care about the painstaking efforts they take to get the facts right. Journalists do this because they view themselves as having a sacred oath of sorts to protect and inform the public.

Teach your children well. When kids cite information they see online, ask them to examine the source of that information, even if it means tracing it back. Help them learn the difference between a legitimate and a questionable source. Walk your children through the steps for figuring out the sources of research studies that are cited, and teach them how large a sample size needs to be for the data to be meaningful.

Consult fact-checkers. Bookmark the watchdog sites mentioned in the graphic on the next page to fact-check political stories. These resources point out when a website is pretending to be a media outlet.

Seeing isn't always believing. Don't assume that you're so sophisticated that you can't be fooled: Pictures often trick people and can be faked just as easily as words can. There are online tools to determine if a photo is not from a recent news event or has been photoshopped or altered in some way. Google Images can help with this: Instead of entering a search term, clicking the camera icon will allow you to search by URL or by an uploaded image. You can then scan the web to hunt for the original image.

Is it actually an ad? Common Sense Media is a trusted resource for teaching young and old how to tell the difference between an ad and a story online. A few red flags: unusual URLs, all-caps text, bold claims, low-quality design, no sources, sexualized content for clickbait (such as women in bikinis), vague or absent "about us" sections. For more from Common Sense Media, visit https://www.commonsensemedia.org.

Exercise parental controls. Teach your children the difference between opinion and fact. Here's a fun, real-time experiment: When siblings argue about the news of the day, assign each of them the duty of researching facts to back up the opinions they're stating (and turn dinnertime diatribes into valuable learning experiences!). If they're doing research for a school project, insist that they ensure their sources are legitimate before citing them, even if that isn't required (upside: extra credit!).

ESCAPE YOUR MEDIA BUBBLE

LEFT | CENTER | RIGHT

ALJAZEERA

the guardian

The New York Times

AP

NATIONAL REVIEW

COLOR LINES

n p r

BBC

Bloomberg
NEWS

THE WALL STREET JOURNAL
WSJ

teen VOGUE

PBS

The Washington Post

THOMSON REUTERS

the weekly Standard

THE NEW YORKER

The Economist

WHO WATCHES THE WATCHERS?

Snopes.com

NiemanLab

MEDIAMATTERS
FOR AMERICA

FACTCHECK.ORG
A PROJECT OF THE ANNENBERG PUBLIC POLICY CENTER

THE CENTER FOR MEDIA JUSTICE

POLITIFACT

PRO PUBLICA

NAVIGATING THE MEDIA LANDSCAPE

Craig Newmark, the founder of Craigslist and the Craig Newmark Foundation, is a leading advocate for "trustworthy journalism." The internet pioneer, philanthropist, and social justice advocate began sharing a curated list of local events with his personal network in 1995, and soon his list expanded into the sprawling classified website known as Craigslist. His business model is powered by his mission to be "doing well by doing good."

Soledad O'Brien is a renowned journalist and documentarian, now founder and CEO of Starfish Media Group (SMG), a multi-platform media production and distribution company. Through SMG, Soledad hosts and produces reports and documentaries for numerous top-tier media outlets, including CNN, HBO, Fox, and NBC. Soledad is also a frequent and sharply observant user of social media, where she not only highlights the contradictions and hypocrisies of political figures but also how the media covers those figures. In addition to being a top global journalist, after being moved by the stories she was reporting from post–Hurricane Katrina New Orleans, Soledad launched her PowHERful Foundation to help put young women through college. Jennifer Pozner uses her media analysis expertise to amplify women, people of color, and non-binary people's voices, power, and visibility in the media. In 2001, she founded Women In Media & News (WIMN), where she advocates for policy reform and systemic changes in all forms of media. The New York City native formerly directed the women's desk at the national media watch group FAIR, where she wrote for *Extra!* magazine and organized their Feminist Coalition on Public Broadcasting.

In a rapidly changing media landscape, it can seem impossible to influence how stories are told by the media and to filter what is truth from what is fiction. We talked to these three media-makers with decades of experience and asked them how media leaders hold themselves and their peers accountable to create and promote credible, inclusive stories and platforms. We asked them to share what they've learned about discernment in the age of *#alternativefacts* and *#fakenews*, and how to build a free and open media that serves all of us. Craig, Soledad, and Jennifer represent a growing community of media professionals working to shift our media ecosystem to reflect the diversity of our population.

"Objectivity is
a myth."
—Jennifer
Pozner

When asked how to influence media outlets, Soledad had some frank advice: "If you want to influence media outlets, calling them is pretty useless. You're just harassing some poor intern. If you insist on calling anyway, calling to vent won't mean anything. Call and have a point or a position they can track. One of the best ways to get them to take notice is actually through your use of social media. The way outlets track audience response now is digitally. They watch what's trending. As a journalist, I also benefit from social media; I feel more informed because of social media. I get much more access to information and stories that I would not have seen before."

As someone who has devoted most of her life to using her words and work to hold the media accountable, Jennifer shares how reaching out to media outlets can help shift the public debate: "Letters to the editor seem to be a dying art, with newspapers folding left and right, but they influence public policy at the local, and sometimes national, level. When media outlets are reporting and running commentary that is factually inaccurate and biased against a group of people, it's imperative that those of us who care about this in our communities make our news outlets understand. Most people will stop at asking for a correction, but we need to ask for follow-up content because [inaccurate and sensational #fakenews] stories like "Mike Brown was a murderer" or "Abortion causes breast cancer" are what people remember; a correction isn't what people remember. We need follow-up commentary that corrects the record in a narrative form. That can get the point across that something covered previously didn't get the whole story."

Craig sees the News Integrity Initiative and social media platforms as antidotes to unreliable media coverage and practices. He said that "they are fully implementing [media accountability] practices, [so] people should be able to choose trustworthy sources and ignore unreliable ones."

Key Points

You have the power to influence the media. Whether you use traditional letter writing, email, or social media, giving feedback to media outlets matters. For maximum impact, be intentional and solution-driven when you contribute a critique or commentary. If in doubt, make a statement—you might just be able to "correct the record."

GET YOUR FACTS STRAIGHT

Traditionally, Journalism 101 students learn the basic components of an article (who, what, where, when, why) and how to determine whether a source is credible by fact-checking claims.

These essentials are the backbone of a good story and integral to delivering the most comprehensive picture possible of what happened. But outside of journalism school, Soledad told us that social media raises the question: "What is 'press'? Social media has turned more people into 'press.' It gave us all access to a lot more 'press' than in the past. The best way to have an impact and be relevant is to get your facts straight. Who are your sources? Make sure you're correct. The more accurate you are—not just data, but understanding communities, issues, nuance, and context—the more you will be delivering important stories.

"What does getting your facts straight mean in practice? The classic journalism rule is that if you have one source telling you something over-the-top, there's a good chance it's not true. On the other hand, when people repeat the same information, or when experts agree—in other words, when there's consensus—then it's more likely to be true. Good reporters never go with information unless two independent sources (two sources with firsthand information) are telling them the same thing. When you don't have your own firsthand sources, then you go to media that doesn't just replicate or repeat what other outlets report. You go to media [outlets] that have independent verification that something is true. It's always best for you to be able to go to the source yourself. But if you can't, at least take your information from someone who has gotten their information verified directly."

For Jennifer, checking the validity of source material goes deeper than simple fact-checking. Her experiences have taught her it is important to factor in who is supplying the facts as we determine how to process them. The insight she gained from a challenging experience taught her that "objectivity is a myth": "It's not about objectivity; it is about ethics. If you are reporting, try to get as many voices as possible, do as much research as you can, have facts, and make sure that Kellyanne Conway is never right [about the existence of so-called alternative facts] and that there are such things as facts that we can report without fear or favor."

Jennifer adds that "objectivity is a false construct that privileges the power structures that have and continue to control the filter of the news, the lens, and whose stories get to be told and heard. Objectivity doesn't exist because every one of us brings our subjectivity to every news story we cover or analyze. Instead of objectivity, we should be striving for fairness. As a reporter, you try to get as many sides of a story as you can. Just because there's a powerful voice, it doesn't mean they are right or wrong. An independent voice is important. A marginalized voice is even more important than the voice of somebody who is outside the impacted community.

"One of the ways that objectivity has been weaponized is that people of color and women are told that we are 'too close' to the stories. My first journalism teacher argued in favor of objectivity from the perspective of an older white man whose objectivity was never questioned. He said I could not be objective about reproductive rights because of my gender. But who knows the truth of those stories more innately and through experience than those affected? Meanwhile, white men with money are considered the only neutral voice in journalism, and that is patently false and an idea that needs to die."

Like Soledad and Jennifer, Craig is committed to upholding the integrity of fact-driven journalism in an increasingly clickbait-focused and sensational headline-driven industry. He wants the News Integrity Initiative to "affect a new normal of trustworthy journalism, but everyone knows that won't be easy. The Trust Project helps define what trustworthy journalism means, but a network of fact checkers is still evolving, and that's required for the watchdog function."

Although he acknowledges that the road ahead won't always be smooth, he has a plan of action: "Research has started to identify and counter bad actors, with good results, but more time is needed to develop a clear path on how best to counter them for the long term. Success involves the identification of consistently trustworthy news organizations, along with help from social media platforms that would help their members identify trustworthy news versus the opposite, often known as 'fake news.'"

> ### Key Points
>
> Determine the credibility of the stories you read by checking for diverse and reliable sources. If you're concerned that a story isn't legitimate, examine whose claims are supported, consider who is making them, and ask yourself what critical voices are either over-amplified or missing.

KNOW WHO OWNS THE MEDIA

When asked how media ownership impacts coverage and content, Craig states that "there have been news organizations that deliberately compromised their reporting to serve profit and power motives, and somewhere internal battles are being fought, like at CNN and the *Wall Street Journal*."

Soledad concedes, "Media companies may have an agenda as to which stories get covered," but at an individual story level, she adds, "I can say that I never felt that any outlet tried to influence how I reported a story. I never had a problem, even if I was reporting things that may have made my bosses uncomfortable. Being independent now has not changed what I do or how I do it."

Soledad's experience aside, Jennifer fights for policy reform and structural changes to mitigate the chilling impact of corporate ownership and the consolidation on news media reporters' and journalists' ability to tell the whole story. She says, "The more media consolidation happens, the less women and people of color are represented. With more consolidation, we get more all-male and more all-white boards as multinational conglomerates expand."

Key Points

Be mindful of how the interests and perspectives of a small and mostly homogenous group of media owners impact coverage and staffing decisions. Having a clear understanding of how the media market works and shifts with consolidation, buyouts, and mergers provides critical insight into how stories are framed, positioned, and propagated.

TAVI GEVINSON

FOUNDER AND EDITOR IN CHIEF OF *ROOKIE* MAGAZINE, WRITER, ACTOR

Tavi Gevinson first made headlines as a feminist, fashion, and pop-culture trend-setter when she started her blog Style Rookie at eleven years old. In 2011, *Rookie* surpassed 1 million views within less than a week of launching and cemented Tavi's status as a media mogul with a singular ability to inspire the next generation and visionaries of all ages.

What's Missing from the Public Conversation?

"When I started Style Rookie, there weren't any publications for teenagers or young women that didn't feel like they were made by adults whose primary motive was profit. I wanted something that was honest, by other teenagers, and actually addressed what my friends and I were going through and experiencing.

"When you're a teenager, your primary relationship to society is as a consumer because you can't vote yet and you don't have much control over your own life. I wanted teenagers to be making things for each other without having ideas for their life handed down by an authority figure like a legacy publication. Now you see mainstream teen magazines promoting and highlighting young voices, which by this point is sort of moot. Teenagers are creating content for each other."

Own Your Bias

"I see a lot of media where everyone needs to be everything for everyone, instead of having a range of people being their best selves and speaking to their own individual experiences.

"You'll have a publication hiring someone as a token and asking them to speak for everyone who looks like them. I encourage specificity in the writers I edit and remind them that they only have to speak for themselves.

"[Novelist and journalist] Joan Didion believed that it's best to establish what your bias is as a writer, as opposed to creating a false objectivity you can't achieve—there's no such thing."

Set Your Rates and Your Standards

"Develop your own intuition and moral compass as to what feels like a compromise, and what is an opportunity to make things possible that weren't possible before. You have to take it case by case and hone your sense of what feels right for you. Some writers and freelancers I know have to write things that feel less than dignified or less complex because that frees up their time to write something longer form and more necessary that can help people."

> "Be okay with the idea that someone might not like you or agree with you."

Respect Your Audience's Intelligence

"The way we all get and receive information is a little more chaotic. But the internet is the same thing that made *Rookie* possible. Everyone has to be responsible for their own filter, and knowing what to trust, and if something is fact-checked or not."

Substance versus Spectacle

"Hyperbole and spectacle are bigger than I realized, and I have seen that my job is not just affirming people, but just trying to be as truthful and measured as possible. This goes back to wanting to create content that's not just disposable and attention-grabbing, but that really makes a difference in people's lives as opposed to functioning as spectacle.

"I used to roll my eyes when there was concern over pop culture and entertainment being distractions because I felt like there are actually good ways to learn through teaching moments, like Kendall Jenner's [controversial] 2017 Pepsi ad.

"Although something like this is important, it can be a distraction from issues that affect people's lives. The world feels more and more like a reality show, and when spectacle succeeds it distracts people from the realities of their own oppression and how to fix that."

Tavis Gevinson's Five Tips

1. Find your own answers, listen to yourself, and think for yourself.

2. Read everything.

3. Be okay with the idea that someone might not like you or agree with you. Keep your list of the five people whose opinions you truly care about and who will call you on your blind spots, and take criticism and praise from elsewhere with a grain of salt.

4. Be willing to go into unknowns and expand your horizons. Expand the types of things you're thinking about and writing about. If people praise you for the same thing over and over, you self-imitate, you don't grow, and you burn out.

5. If you're a writer and you write one personal essay, you can exploit that part of yourself over and over—do what you gotta do to make that money—but your own growth should always come first.

Every day, people become inspired by a great cause and start their own groups to address it. A lofty goal for sure, but burnout is inevitable without the correct mindset, collective, and strategy. The people we interviewed here developed their voices, missions, and lives' work through experimentation— all the while revealing solutions to problems without losing steam. Nothing was known in the beginning, but all was revealed in the doing. This "git 'er done" attitude, combined with bravery and a willingness to embrace constant change with a sense of humor and humanity, is the key to success here. Listening to others, keeping a close eye on what works, and discarding what doesn't is a tactic for sustainability. With great influence comes great responsibility—and these tales of leadership are born of hard-won experience. We spoke to a diverse group of inspired advocates to share stories of adventure, success, and even danger from the trenches.

NONPROFIT AND ADVOCACY GROUP FOUNDER WISDOM

Chuck Swift is the former deputy CEO of the Sea Shepherd Conservation Society, an international nonprofit marine wildlife conservation organization that employs direct-action tactics to investigate, document, and confront illegal activities on the high seas. Pamela Hadfield is a founding member of HelloMD.com, the largest online medical cannabis community in the United States, destigmatizing cannabis, helping shepherd it to the mainstream, and bringing the latest medical and tech breakthroughs to the forefront. Dr. Geoffrey Tabin is the cofounder of Himalayan Cataract Project (HCP), a nonprofit bringing world-class eye care to the needlessly blind in the developing world.

If you're reading this book, you've been activated and filled with passion and purpose. But before you create an activist group, you need to take a look at yourself, learn the basics, set up your base camp, and head out from there. We spoke to these three social-impact superheroes about how they found their life's work by recognizing a need, and figuring out a more innovative and creative way to get from point A to point B, rapidly bypassing existing systems and creating new ones. In doing so, they provide a blueprint to move energy from thought to action.

CHUCK SWIFT, ECO-WARRIOR

Soldier, activist, grassroots entrepreneur, and eco-warrior Chuck Swift has lived a life of action, adventure, intermittent income, sacrificed relationships, and also starred in Animal Planet's popular *Whale Wars* show, captaining the *Bob Barker*. The show documented the Sea Shepherd Conservation Society as it interfered with Japanese "research" whaling activities in Antarctica (which Sea Shepherd claims are a cover for illegal commercial whaling).

In 1990, Swift had his aha moment when facing a bulldozer: "My first protest, and within minutes I was knee-deep in dirt before a massive bulldozer, questioning my resolve. I was shaking in fear. About twenty-five of us were protesting clear-cuts actively destroying some of the oldest trees in the world—the Humboldt Redwoods. We ended up zip-tied and booked into the county jail—but we had stopped them, temporarily. I was forever hooked on making a difference.

"There's no manual to getting started. You have to *do* it. The key to being an effective executive is to execute: projects, budgets, whatever the task. The root word of *activist* is *active*, and that is what you should be: whether as a minister who tends to the poor, a teacher who weaves ethics into lessons, or a consumer voting with your dollars. While I have always chosen what some folks consider the more out-on-a-limb strategies, tactics, and organizations, I feel it's crucial to acknowledge the power of activism within our daily lives and give it a workout. If someone makes a sexist joke . . . are you active enough to act?

"We can't all be expected to be frontline activists, getting arrested monthly, sinking illegal whaling boats, and chaining ourselves to trees. It takes all kinds—support and determination from all segments of society—working together in so many little ways—to form a solid defense (and perhaps cohesive offense) against the corporate and political interests that want to squash our future."

What Are You Willing to Trade Off?

Many of us live our lives in relative safety and believe that if you can dream it, you can be it. But how many are willing to commit to choosing a course and staying on it, even if we know that the choices we make are irreversible?

Having spoken with many "Save the [fill in the blank]" activist leaders out there, it's clear that taking a stand against tyranny can have consequences that last forever. A criminal record, an FBI file as a person of interest, being flagged at airports, and perhaps difficulty finding employment in non-activist jobs; these can be the norm. Welcome to the front lines of life-changing activism.

Swift notes, "I've gone years at a time with no real 'life.' Every weekend a protest or prep meeting. Sacrificing finances and relationships, risking freedoms and personal security, because for me, it was worth it. I've seen the results of some of the things I've done—but I always contemplated the potential results of what I was doing before I committed. You can't put yourself on the line and expect no risk. It boils down to this: *How much risk are you willing to take? What is the potential reward (accomplishment/impact)? What do you think are your realistic odds of achieving your objectives?* If you're not willing to take the risk, don't cross the line.

"There are many ways to be effective. You'll certainly find a method that suits your comfort and risk level. The movement needs attorneys, cooks, welders, engineers, artists, writers, bookkeepers, CPAs, and MBAs. Figure out a way to apply your strengths to a worthy cause and build that community. Don't underestimate the revolutionary value of quality parenting or engagement in local and civil issues in your own neighborhood. The world is a crazy place, and whether or not we win the large battles, hunker down in your own region. Build networks of caring, skilled, diverse, trustworthy people—including future generations—and sow the seeds of the future and of revolution. There's no reason for most people to risk encounters with law enforcement, but if you want to go to the next level, study. Just like you'd practice a new skill of any kind, determine what skills you'll need for the activities you wish to pursue, and in the (increasingly hard-to-find) privacy of your space, read, learn, practice, and prepare beforehand. Choose your targets carefully, lest you become one." For more on Sea Shepherd Conservation Society, visit https://seashepherd.org.

Key Points

Self-awareness and knowing where you fit into the revolution is the key to starting any effort. So before you head out with your protest sign, look inward to see what level of activist and risk-taker you are comfortable being and what you are willing to trade off.

PAMELA HADFIELD: WEED WARRIOR

Many are called to the cannabis space because of personal experience, a belief in the healing properties of the plant, and an understanding that pain management in the United States is turning into an opioid epidemic. Pamela Hadfield is no different, and no stoner: She's a tech entrepreneur who suffered from debilitating migraines and was unwilling to spend the rest of her life numbed out on Vicodin. A "weed warrior" was born, and Pamela realized that if she could help herself, she could help others.

Pamela's journey was the impetus for HelloMD.com, the most successful online health and wellness community within the cannabis industry with more than 100,000 members. Pamela weighs in on how to build that kind of healthcare revolution from the ground up: "HelloMD has been an evolution and a fast-moving work in progress since Day One, informed by both by my personal health-care experience and the founding team's collective years in business and technology. The cannabis industry sits still for no one. Between the shifting nature of regulations at the state and federal levels and the swift growth of a new and burgeoning industry, it's unlike any other industry I've worked in. To survive, you must be fast, nimble, flexible, and smart.

"HelloMD offers live video doctor consultations to patients online for medical marijuana recommendations within the states of California and New York. This approach, called telehealth or telemedicine, is legal in one form or another in most states within the United States. This is a progressive and positive direction within mainstream medicine, as it increases access to health care, and the need for a doctor's consultation when it comes to cannabis is no different.

Key Points

Building a company based on listening to what a patient wants and needs can be truly revolutionary, especially compared to traditional medicine and Big Pharma.

"We began to hear from patients that they valued the convenience and low price point telehealth afforded them, as consultations and medicine are not covered by insurance. Privacy is also important to most people seeking a medical marijuana recommendation, because the stigma is alive and well. Finally, telehealth is critical for patients who are homebound due to illness.

"We started by thinking of the journey of the patient into the world of cannabis: It's a confusing marketplace after patients receive their recommendation.

Patients advised us on what they needed and defined our next steps. In addition to offering educational content, we decided to shift our business into the realm of community, allowing patients to ask questions on our site for doctors, nurses, and

community to answer. We realized we needed to close the loop and offer an online marketplace for patients to purchase their cannabis products."

Connecting Community in a Shifting Landscape
With the government frequently changing the laws around cannabis, Pamela is focused on the big picture: "The cannabis industry is like no other in that we're severely restricted in how we talk to patients. Traditional advertising and marketing outlets are closed to cannabis businesses. We engage with brands and retailers directly, affording patients the opportunity to learn more about them without ever having to walk into a marijuana dispensary. From a disruptive standpoint, this is not a California-only or United States–only market, but a global marketplace and movement. Medical consultations and recommendations are needed across the globe, and patients need to be served. We're ready." For more information, visit https://www.hellomd.com.

DR. GEOFFREY TABIN: WARRIOR FOR THE SIGHTLESS

Dr. Geoffrey Tabin has an ambitious plan: wiping out blindness in his lifetime with the Himalayan Cataract Project. He came to his calling twenty years ago while mountaineering in the Himalayas. He witnessed a Dutch medical team perform cataract surgery, and it inspired him and cofounder Dr. Sanduk Ruit to deliver a life-changing surgery to hundreds of thousands of people around the globe and prevent needless blindness. They don't just fly in and fly out: They teach, train, and help develop the skills of local doctors, nurses, and technicians. They leave behind the medical equipment that they bring for the local medical team. The traveling doctors have to wrestle with sometimes-hostile governments and local officials who may block their work out of fear or ego. Being a health warrior is not always welcomed by the powers that be, even if the intentions of the medical team are pure. These doctors believe that the healing power they've been granted needs to be used to help those less fortunate—and they are hell-bent on making that happen.

Tabin notes, "The ability to so deeply and positively affect the course of another human's existence on the planet with your hands, a few instruments, and a finely honed surgical intuition is a tremendous privilege. The project was accelerated by critical surgical technique advancements, the availability of intraocular lenses, and my love of the Himalayan region of Nepal. The surgical techniques allowed us to do faster and more efficient surgery with fewer complications in the developing world. These new lenses allowed patients to see better almost immediately after the surgery."

> ### Key Points
>
> When you listen to people, meet their needs, and solve their problems, you build a more powerful community, create a more sustainable model, and set an example for your industry.

Necessity Is the Mother of Efficiency

Most Americans know that dealing with health insurance companies is soul-numbing and time-consuming. Most doctors feel the same way—it keeps them from what they would prefer to be doing: spending time with patients. Medical volunteerism has its own mother lode of red tape. Many doctors file it under the "life's too short" category because of insurance companies.

Tabin says, "In traditional medicine, we spend 60 percent of our time filling out forms, billing, and charting. U.S. regulatory hurdles slow down everything outside of the actual surgery, which is quite fast (six minutes or so per cataract). We have large teams that work in an assembly-line fashion with the goal of getting the patient to the operating table of the surgeon. Charting is done, but a scribe will do this for the surgeon, and as a surgeon you focus on one task.

> ### Key Points
>
> Building efficient teams and processes helps you move fast and gets you right to the real work.

"Our patients will leave their homes in the mountains and be lead blindly (literally) for six days to visit you—we deliver the same high-quality care to every case. This information spreads by word of mouth. We have also set up very efficient processes to teach others these systems. We work hard, and that's highly contagious: The people who join our teams are thrilled to be working alongside us and get wrapped up in the goals of treating everyone who shows up."

Navigating the Nuances

Global success means local know-how: where to source supplies, how to deal with foreign licenses, how to get through hurdles, and then how to build on that experience and expand. If you are looking to start your own medical volunteer group, take a page from Team HCP and don't reinvent the wheel.

Per Tabin, "We get around Big Medicine, NGOs (nongovernmental organizations), government borders, and try to sidestep red tape to be nimble. We make our own lenses in Nepal or buy them at a fraction of the cost from India. We buy antibiotics from India. We deal with foreign medical boards by obtaining a license to practice in the various countries where we work before going. It is a risk we take, and we always try to practice very safe care, particularly when we put kids under general anesthesia (always with an anesthesiologist present). We don't bill insurance, so that's one less hassle. We mostly cross borders with a passport and a visa like everyone else.

"Bringing medical supplies is challenging: Customs officials have confiscated equipment and supplies, even after we explain that we are there to help and provide care for people. We spread essentials out across multiple pieces of luggage and have the team members bring the supplies in the hopes that someone will get through with enough. We also use multiple small bags so as not to draw attention. I like to place candy on top of my supplies because there is nothing more distracting—other than porn."

> **Key Points**
>
> Work the system to find unexpected routes to the result you want.

The Work Behind the Work

A price tag is attached to all this benevolence, and it isn't cheap from a time or money perspective. Consider your network, your net worth, and your financially independent friends or companies looking to pitch in for a good cause before you decide to hang out your volunteer shingle. Reflect on your own ability to stand for ten hours in a sweltering operating room on a diet of mystery stew. Do you have what it takes? Let's see. . . .

According to Tabin, "We started with fundraising, then organizing and purchasing supplies, finding international partners, assembling a team and equipment, working with local health officials in the destination country, organizing transport for patients, organizing food for patients, finding a suitable hospital. It's very detail-oriented work that takes months.

"We raise money from some of our stateside patients who often take an interest in this work and make contributions, as well as some USAID grant money.

"This work not only feels good, but it also seems only right to give back to a society that spent resources training you. A few years ago I wrote guidelines for who we would work with: surgeons willing to pay for and sit on a long flight, work really hard all day in a sweltering operating theater, go back to a spartan room after dinner, and then repeat, all on their precious vacation time. We do this work without pay when we could be at home with our families, because it means so much to us and it is a part of who we are.

"The goal would be to treat the 20 million people worldwide with reversible cataract blindness. There are those who are in war-torn and unstable countries that we can't risk getting teams to, but we can make a very meaningful dent in this number with the proper funding and team development."

ART AND ADVOCACY
EMBRACING CREATIVE ACTIVISM AS A CAREER

Josh MacPhee is a successful activist, artist, and cofounder at Justseeds Artist's Cooperative who manages to prolifically publish while raising a two-year-old in Brooklyn, New York. Paul C. Ha is the director of the List Visual Arts Center at Massachusetts Institute of Technology (MIT).

Josh and Paul chronicle and document social justice movements and provide a peek into how they pull it off, and why there's no time like the present to show and tell. This is "git 'er done" advice from two career creatives who make it happen from the streets to the museum.

"Making it" as a creative looks pretty sexy on TV, if the lifestyle of the agency crew of *Mad Men* is any indication, but the work of social justice promotion through art is anything but. Being an activist artist can be financially challenging and without the glitz and martinis of a classic ad-agency career. Bottom line: What goes on in today's world needs to be documented and showcased beyond the lens of media. If Shepard Fairey's Barack Obama "Hope" poster is any indication of an ongoing trend, the art of the resistance has bubbled up from the people and infiltrated popular culture.

HISTORICAL PERSPECTIVE

Effective propaganda art is simple: It outlines the principles of the group with DIY style and methods. Historically, these posters, flags, and banners of movements served as a call to action for oppressed people. Color blocking, powerful typography, and visual concepts identified and understood from a distance (whether the viewer could read it or not) are hallmarks of activist artwork.

Josh MacPhee, who teaches a propaganda art history course called "Agit-Prop" at the Pratt Institute, goes further: "Every major social upheaval or revolution over the past century has been accompanied by a massive outpouring of art and culture. Study and learn what works. Whether it's the Mexican or Russian Revolution, the U.S. civil rights movement, worker or student revolts in the 1960s and '70s, the South African anti-apartheid movement, the Arab Spring, Occupy, Black Lives Matter, or the fight against pipelines on indigenous lands, every one has seen explosions of creativity and culture as a form of communicating the demands of the movements."

AN ARTIST BECOMES ACTIVATED

Josh weighs in on what activated him: "I can't remember a time I wasn't making art. As a teen, I joined the DIY punk music community: writing, designing, and publishing zines; making t-shirts, record covers, and concert flyers for my friends' bands. The punk scene was highly politicized: I started making political posters and other art for activist groups. Punk rock is built around art and culture. It could be a playground to explore different ways of thinking and being, and a tool in imagining (and showing) a better life."

Moving passion to action in this crowd is about collaboration, so Josh founded a community of the top social justice artists in the United States that operates from two platforms he created:

Per Josh, "Justseeds.org is a cooperative of twenty-nine activated artists that exists at the cross-section of art, cooperative economic experimentation, social justice, and personal expression in concert with collective action. The group produces graphics for grassroots struggles for justice, works collaboratively, and wheatpastes posters on the streets—all while building community.

"Interference Archive is a volunteer-run hub focused on the cultural and political production of social movements with four exhibitions and seventy public events a year. We aggregate more than five dozen artists, designers, archivists, and activists who help run the space. We develop the idea that art and culture are central to our lives, and connected to social justice. As communities, we're always in motion, always organizing to improve ourselves, and the culture we produce is central to understanding who we have been, who we are, and who we can become."

For more on Justseeds and Interference Archive, visit https://www.justseeds.org and www.interferencearchive.org, respectively.

OUR PAST, OUR FUTURE, OUR CULTURE

Protest art travels from the streets to the hallowed halls of our nation's museums, and Paul C. Ha of the MIT List Visual Arts Center is at the helm of trying to save our unique American protest history in his museum's recent retrospective *Civil Disobedience*—"a program of documentaries, news footage, citizen journalism, artists' films, and videos focusing on the moment of political resistance and public demonstration from the early twentieth century through today."

Paul says the challenge as a museum director is that, despite any personal point of view, "as a nonprofit you can't be political, but you can reveal the history of a situation from all sides and hope people are woke enough to face reality— our current situation can take us back sixty years. Social justice is a pendulum moving in one direction and sometimes swinging further back. Activated people want to make the current administration aware this is not what we want."

Cutting arts funding across the board disadvantages arts organizations in smaller cities and rural areas. The local Shakespeare Company or theater group, the small ballet troupes, these organizations rely on the monetary assistance and stamp of approval from the NEA and NEH. Most of the larger metropolitan areas will likely have private donors willing and able to support the arts. Just like Josh, Paul believes that art is for everyone, defines our country, and shows where we've been and where we're going.

Paul expands, saying, "Art is important for society and movements, but the NEA and NEH now have zeroed-out budgets. A town without art becomes culturally impoverished. Great societies are valuated by the culture they leave behind. Cutting art budgets in towns and schools creates a fear of culture and feeds the current administration, which frames art funding as benefiting the 'coastal elite.' Cutting funding steals from children and their future: Science museums, aquariums, and libraries across the country suffer. Art and culture are rooted in creativity, and because they make you think about issues, there's a fear of culture in the current administration. We do not want to be the decade that had no culture, and America's museums are the place to document our journey." For more on the MIT List Visual Arts Center, visit https://lightart.mit.edu.

Paul C. Ha's Five Thought-Starters for Creatives

1. We can't make people change, but what we can do is cause people to react. Changes come with individual and collective reactions and actions.

2. We need to react to the election and reveal how people have reacted to civil disobedience historically.

3. The internet helps everyone participate and interact with art.

4. Change happens when you put sunshine on issues. We present all sides, show what was going on historically, and highlight the important ideas that motivated the movements.

5. Americans have a right to enjoy culture in their towns and schools—to be part of the larger cultural creatives!

HOW TO MAKE THE MOST OF ONLINE PETITIONS

Another day, another online petition. You get emails urging you to sign on; you see them shared on Facebook. Online petitions are easy—frictionless even—to set up, and it can feel great to shout your values from the digital rooftop by creating or signing them. But have you ever wondered whether they have an impact or not?

The answer is . . . *maybe*. Any time an online petition gets a significant number of signatures it indicates that at the very least it's raised awareness about the topic at hand—and that's a great thing. Awareness doesn't always translate into tangible change, but you can be sure change won't happen if people don't know about the problem. Successful petitions apply pressure.

So how do you make your online petition stand out?

MAKE IT COMPELLING

Start with a great personal story. The personal story doesn't necessarily have to be about you, but it should be an identifiably human (or animal) story.

Share why it resonates with you. If the story isn't yours, you can still share why it touches you so much that you're asking your personal network to raise its voice. The more you care, the more they'll care.

Build empathy. Share relatable details. Allow people to imagine it could happen to them. Share pictures to show whom you're trying to help.

Provide examples. Let's say you want to start an online petition opposing a toxic waste facility being built nearby. There's a place for the stats about the correlation between proximity to such sites and poorer health outcomes, but grab people right away by telling the story of one child's struggle with asthma (and how it reminds you of your father's losing battle with emphysema). Share how the child can no longer go out and play, recalling times we've all felt left out. Pulling on the heartstrings? Certainly. Authentic individual outcome of decisions made far away by people who never have to meet that kid? Also true. And fair game.

MAKE IT URGENT

It's right, but why right now? Explain why the petition is needed now. Is there a deadline for public comment on a proposed government policy? Is there a city council meeting coming up where a relevant decision will be made? Give people a reason to sign right now.

Why should we use our outside voices? Let your network know why you need their support, and why you need them to share it. Why is it something you can't handle privately? Why do you need backup? Let people know that they (in large numbers) can make a difference.

MAKE IT INSPIRING

Give people the satisfaction of a potential solution. There's a place for solutionless ranting. But when it comes to an online petition that people want to sign and share (which is critical to having the petition raise a lot of awareness), asking for a specific action or change will make your petition more appealing to more people, more credible to its targets, and a better story for media.

⬡ TOOLS FOR THE TASK

Care2 petitions

https://www.thepetitionsite.com/create-a-petition.html

https://www.thepetitionsite.com/how-to-write-a-petition/

Change.org

https://change.org/start-a-petition

https://guide.change.org

GoPetition

https://www.gopetition.com/start-a-petition

https://www.gopetition.com/how-to-write-a-petition

iPetitions

https://www.ipetitions.com

https://www.ipetitions.com/guide

MoveOn Petitions

https://petitions.moveon.org

https://petitions.moveon.org/campaign_tips.html

We the People (White House petitions):

https://petitions.whitehouse.gov

Think big, yet practical. The problem is probably big. The solution should also be big. Even if you're asking for a first step in what will inevitably be a series of steps toward an ultimate solution, let people know the big idea you're fighting for—and the achievable ask you have right now.

MAKE IT A MOVEMENT

Social media for the win! Make sure to refer to page 11 for tips about spreading the word using social media.

Turn signers into superfans. Most petition sites let you update signers during and after the process. Let them know about milestones reached, and then keep them informed as you push forward. If your petition is part of a larger effort or organization, you now have a group of people who share your values and want to help. Keep them posted. Keep them invested. Keep them raising their voices.

From the Mouths of Organizers

BUILDING SUSTAINABLE GRASSROOTS ORGANIZATIONS

Amber Goodwin is founding director of Community Justice Reform Coalition, which describes itself as a national advocacy coalition that promotes and invests in evidence-based policies and programs to prevent gun violence and uplift criminal justice reforms in urban communities of color. Eli Erlick is director and cofounder of Trans Student Educational Resources (TSER), the only national organization run by transgender youth and focusing on trans students. TSER has more than a dozen programs and services ranging from creating model policies to Trans Youth Leadership Summit, the only national fellowship program for young trans organizers, which fosters a new generation of transgender excellence. Eli is currently a PhD student researching the political philosophy of the transgender movement. Majora Carter is CEO of the Majora Carter Group.

Majora focuses her energies on transforming communities as a real estate developer and a technology company founder, creating both beautiful spaces and job opportunities where they are needed most. Majora started out as a leading urban revitalization strategist, creating and implementing numerous green infrastructure projects and policies through founding Sustainable South Bronx.

As you move from caring about an issue to activating to address it to organizing other people to join you, you may find yourself (sometimes accidentally) being an "organizer." No matter how much you care, no matter how exciting the initial progress is, no matter how much other people say they'll help carry the load, being an organizer can often feel frustrating, thankless, and exhausting. We asked this trio of organizers what got them going and keeps them going.

THE SPARK OF ADVOCACY: "I CAN ADD VALUE HERE"

Being of value and service can often spark advocacy, as it did for Majora: "I wasn't an athletic or musical kid. All I had was a brain, and I was creative. I knew I was going to college, and part of that was I wanted to get out of my neighborhood. After I graduated, I met some folks who had started an arts organization, and I loved what they were doing, but I hadn't even realized it was in my neighborhood. I realized I needed to spend more time there, and that was when we discovered the city's plan to build a huge waste facility there. At this point, I took a good look around and realized no one was looking at this, and I thought, 'I can definitely add value here.' I knew it was just the beginning. If we could pull it off, then what else could we do? I began to look into what else was missing to make the community a place where we'd all want to live. That's when I started looking into economic development."

Stepping into a void that should be filled is a common instigator for many who begin grassroots organizing. It may come after years of firsthand experience that reinforces the need for someone willing to do the work. For Eli, these experiences began in childhood. She says, "I first opened up about being transgender when I was eight years old, in the third grade. I spent the next five years being completely rejected and targeted by my community. I experienced isolation, harassment, and beatings frequently during my time in grade school. I still consider myself lucky because my family allowed me to transition when I was thirteen. Shortly after, I met other trans people for the first time. These experiences of both violence and community-building led me to think that it is possible to undo the systemic harm trans people face while also fostering connections with one another. I realized that it was my responsibility to help make the lives of trans people better everywhere and that it is imperative to educate those around me on transgender issues. I cofounded Trans Student Educational Resources when I was sixteen, a junior in high school. There was no one else taking on this work, and somebody had to do it."

Stepping into a gap can also be about representation as much as it is about the action, and Amber was conscious of bringing both to the table: "The biggest catalyst for my starting the Community Justice Reform Coalition was the shooting that happened in Charleston in 2015. Seeing firsthand the pure hatred that came from someone who disliked people who shared my skin color was profound. Even so, I did not dive right in when I got outraged about gun violence in America. I went and asked who else could be or was already working on this issue, and I realized that not many other people of color were starting this type of organization. I prayed a lot, asked for discernment, and decided to move forward with forming CJRC. It was a really hard move to make—from idea to reality to paycheck to sustainability."

> **Key Points**
>
> Create the organization you wish you could join but can't find. Not only will you be filling a void, you will be creating something you are passionate about and committed to.

CATCHING FIRE: GIVING COMMUNITIES A VOICE

One of Majora's challenges was (and still is) to inspire people to attach value to themselves and their community when they are used to seeing it dismissed and devalued: "Most people were so demoralized that they thought, 'What do you expect? This is the South Bronx,' and I was horrified to hear that. But you looked around and there were no beautiful places, even after there were no longer abandoned buildings." So Majora started doing focus groups and events and really listening to people to learn what kind of community they wanted to live in. Turns out they wanted parks and green spaces and jobs—just like any community would. Majora also found and reached out to organizations that were already known and trusted in the neighborhood.

Sometimes grassroots organizing begins in the neighborhood, but Eli's experience is an example of the internet becoming a virtual neighborhood for a community that is geographically isolated. "I made trans friends online," she says. "I lived in a rural community and was the only person who was publicly trans at the time. Every trans student I've ever met has been denied at least one basic right. Access to restrooms, being called by the correct name, or having easily available lifesaving medicine can be luxuries within our community. I know I have been denied all of those at least once, and it's worse for many others. When we are denied these necessities, we are motivated to take action and ask for more: for liberation. When I was fifteen, I started to speak with other trans teens about creating a project by and for us. We know what is best for our own community and we are capable of taking action ourselves."

Respecting that communities know what's best for them and must be part of any solution is also central to Amber's approach: "I build community around the idea of helping to reduce gun violence by going to the people who are most impacted by violence and asking them what they need or want to be successful. Having self-determination on what happens to our communities is key to people of color and to organizing." Respecting those already doing the work is another critical value. Amber maintains, "Part of CJRC's charge is to help build community and support for the communities impacted by violence. Another part of our work is to make sure we are developing and supporting existing and new leaders working on gun violence prevention for the long term. CJRC has two goals: to reduce gun-related homicides and to reduce mass incarceration—we want to partner with groups that were mission-aligned with the same philosophy. I identify potential partners by talking to leaders or organizations already doing the work of supporting communities of color."

> "If we could pull it off, then what else could we do?"
> —Majora Carter

Key Points

Treat your community with respect. Give community members a voice. Be someone who really listens. They will never forget it.

Change is hard, and you may encounter a challenge in the form of resistance along the way. Or, as Majora did, you may have folks wonder why you're focusing on one issue instead of another. If you're lucky, those who resist will ignore you. Majora explains, "When you stick your neck out and try anything new, you run the risk of people looking at you and saying, 'Who does she think she is?' Meet people where they are—sometimes they'll respect it and sometimes they won't. It was clear some folks had no confidence in me, but what they did was leave me alone. Nine months later, when the first phase of the park opened, those resistant people showed up and they were surprised at what we had accomplished—and I shared credit. It was my first act of political diplomacy."

Another challenge that any grassroots organizer should expect is found in fundraising. For Eli, this challenge was intensified by her relative youth. She states, "Fundraising is difficult as a youth-led organization. We are seen as less legitimate and less worthy of donations. We've been fortunate to receive grants, especially from transgender-led foundations, including Trans Justice Funding Project and the Fund for Trans Generations, which have sustained us the past few years. We are also seeing more individual donations as we continue to grow and demonstrate the national influence we have had on the trans community." Amber's fundraising challenges have multiple drivers, which she faces head-on, both by being disciplined with her time and attention and by getting expert help. She says, "Many times people of color or Black folks are not raised to fundraise aggressively, so asking for money has been an issue in the past. First, I manage having the time to fundraise by prioritizing a limited number of buckets of work goals. They are the only buckets in which I allocate my time. I also hired a grant manager (a year in) to help bring in both small and mid-level donors from my friend network."

Key Points

Not everyone is going to support you from the get-go. Not everyone will take you seriously. Not everyone will believe you're in it for the long haul. Take the small wins and use them to chip away at resistance and build coalitions.

Leaders like Eli are often motivated by belief in a big vision. As she says, "It is through imagining a better future that I will continue to work toward transgender justice every day of my life." Motivating others to stick with the journey is often rooted in giving them a sense of self-determination, especially in a day-to-day life that offers so many challenges. As Eli describes, "Every moment of living as a trans person, we have to defend our very existence. Every moment of living as a trans person is being an activist. It's difficult to motivate people, especially young trans people who already have to navigate so much in their lives. I like to motivate the youth we work with by discussing projects each would like to take on. We support them through funding and institutional backing, and that often helps them to self-determine their involvement."

> **Key Points**
>
> Celebrate achieving incremental goals on your way to achieving an inspiring vision. Share the road map, ask for directions, and make sure to refuel when needed.

When it comes to sustaining a grassroots organization, balancing the big vision with incremental achievable goals helps people celebrate small wins but understand the need to keep going. For Eli and TSER this has meant evolving their services by and for the trans community, but it has also meant seeing their work as part of a larger liberation movement. Eli continues, "Originally, when I was a teenager, TSER was primarily focused on policy advocacy. When I was finally able to enact a policy in my school district, yet realized that the harassment I faced continued (albeit in different ways), I knew that we had to build a transformational movement rather than merely reforming what existed. We had to change minds, not bodies. Our belief—liberation for all people—is a set of principles that must be maintained and nurtured. All oppression is connected. By doing what we can to work alongside other groups, we are forging relationships that will incite widespread change across the country for all social movements. To free any community is to free all communities."

When Majora wants to motivate others to join her and to think about their future in a positive, proactive way, she often turns to this well-known quote from *The Little Prince,* by Antoine de Saint-Exupéry, to remind herself that the folks working with you need that big vision too: "If you want to build a ship, don't drum up the men to gather wood, divide the work, and give orders. Instead, teach them to yearn for the vast and endless sea."

Sustainability also requires keeping yourself motivated and healthy, and not putting yourself last. Majora's experience is not unusual among passionate organizers: "Early on it was just sheer force of will. I was doing the best that I could, but I think I was really bad to my own body. I wasn't taking care of myself spiritually either. I wasn't looking at myself as the fabulous person that God created—I didn't feel fabulous at all. If we're responsible for building a really beautiful space for people in God's image, then I should be taking better care of myself and the people around me."

Self-motivation requires every dimension of self-care, including emotional and intellectual. Amber keeps connected to her goals by making sure to listen to and understand the teachings of people of color and marginalized communities. Reading their words motivates Amber because, as she points out, "There is so much on the line to support and amplify those that cannot do that themselves because their/our voices have been silenced." Amber reads "Letter from Birmingham Jail" by Martin Luther King Jr. at least once a week for inspiration and reinvigoration of her foundational principles.

Amber brings both historical context and a big vision for the future to the table to motivate others. "It is hard to get people involved and to care. I believe it is because American society has othered people who do not fit its standards—including those that are survivors of gun violence. I motivate people during setbacks by talking about the long game and also giving context for how far we have to go as people of color in this country. We have come a long way but have an even longer journey to reach liberation for people of color and marginalized communities."

School is the first institution of which most of us are conscious. Until we exit school, it is where we spend the most hours in our day. As parents and community members, we are all served by schools where our children are safe and treated equitably.

INFLUENCING AND IMPROVING CAMPUS SEXUAL ASSAULT POLICIES

Amy Ziering is a two-time Emmy Award–winning and Academy Award–nominated documentary filmmaker. Her most recent film, *The Hunting Ground*, about campus sexual assault, won the Producers Guild of America's Stanley Kramer Award and was shortlisted for an Oscar. Her previous film, *The Invisible War*, a groundbreaking investigation into the epidemic of rape in our military, won the Audience Award at Sundance, two Emmy Awards for Best Documentary and Outstanding Investigative Journalism, and was nominated for an Oscar. The film spurred secretary of defense Leon Panetta to announce policy changes and catalyzed the passing of thirty-five pieces of legislation. She is the recipient of the Néstor Almendros Award for Courage in Filmmaking, the Ridenhour Documentary Film Prize, the Gracie Award for Outstanding Producer, and a Peabody Award.

ASKING THE RIGHT QUESTIONS

Amy notes, "It's not easy to figure out what your college's sexual assault policy is. You have to ask a lot of questions. The problem is that there's no one uniform mandate that all schools have to follow. And they have a vested interest in not letting you know what's going on."

So ask good questions, like these that Amy suggests:

- What are your sexual assault response policies?

- How do you investigate these crimes?

- How do you ensure the process is unbiased?

- How do you support survivors?

- What specific resources are available?

- How many students have you expelled for assault
  in the last decade?

Ask these questions early and often. Call and ask the admissions office. Or the Title IX office. Ask during campus tours. Make sure to tie your interest in these questions (and the answers) to your consideration of whether to attend the college or send your child there. While ownership of the policy may live in various offices of the university, Amy advises everyone to "get on the radar of the Admissions Office—they're accountable. They need to get the message that parents care about this issue and very much want it properly addressed."

Amy's Four Steps to Protect Yourself or Your Kids

1. Watch *The Hunting Ground,* her documentary on campus sexual assault: It's packed with important information you simply cannot get anywhere else.

2. Always know the provenance of your alcohol: There is a lot of mixing of alcohol with other substances, which puts students in much more vulnerable positions.

3. Take a page out of the Mothers Against Drunk Driving (MADD) book and, when going to parties, assign a designated sober friend to keep an eye on friends who are drinking.

4. Have your sons take a bystander intervention course that shows them how to safely and effectively intervene in situations that seem suspect.

One very basic thing we all can do is believe survivors. Responding with understanding and compassion not only helps survivors heal more quickly, but also would lead to society improving its criminal response.

Amy also pointed out that this is a serial-predator crime. A small percentage of men commit these crimes. So, if we can apply pressure on schools to implement better policies, including more accountability for perpetrators, and if we can educate college students to take more steps to protect themselves and their friends, we can reduce the ubiquity of these crimes.

According to Amy, "Many of these colleges are renowned research institutions, but they are remarkably uncurious about compiling statistics when it comes to these crimes on their campuses. We found that often, for various reasons, the stats they do present are wildly inaccurate."

REALITY CHECK

Amy has a vision for more optimal campus sexual assault policies that would reframe this issue and better protect students. These fixes would include:

- A fair and unbiased investigation, adjudication, and accountability process
- Greater support services for survivors, including access to adequate (and long-term) therapy, when necessary
- Efforts to encourage a culture that supports survivors and doesn't tolerate sexual harassment or gender discrimination

SENATOR KIRSTEN GILLIBRAND'S TOP FIVE TIPS

Senator Kirsten Gillibrand is leading the fight to reform the justice system for sexual assault survivors both in the military and on college campuses. In 2013, as chair of the Senate Armed Services Subcommittee on Personnel, she held the first Senate hearing on the issue of sexual assault in the military in almost a decade. She has built a bipartisan coalition of senators in support of her bill, the Military Justice Improvement Act, which would remove sexual assault cases from the chain of command. She has also built a broad, bipartisan coalition for the Campus Accountability and Safety Act, which would finally hold colleges accountable for sexual assault on their campuses. Here are her five recommendations for how to address the campus sexual assault problem as parents, students, and concerned Americans.

1. **Ask students, not just school administration.** Ask school administration questions about campus policy and statistics, but don't skip the campus visit, and ask current students too—both men and

women. Ask what the climate is like. What is the social scene like? Is there a heavy focus on parties? Are there sexual assaults, and do they get reported? If not, why not? Ask the administration about policy, but find out about culture from the people who go to school there.

2. **Ask whether schools have or plan to assign a confidential advisor for sexual assault survivors.** A confidential advisor (who is not a mandated reporter) is a campus resource for survivors. Someone in this role would know the process and all of the survivor's options after an assault. They would also find out and share information on what happens next. There typically is not a one-stop shop for survivors. For example, sometimes a student might want accommodation to avoid their assailant, and only a school can make such accommodations. Law enforcement can't do it. However, there should be a relationship between a school and law enforcement so that if a survivor decides to report to local law enforcement, they get treated well. A college can help with that.

3. **Stay in it for the long haul.** Senator Gillibrand has lately spent time researching the women's suffrage movement at the turn of the twentieth century. For example, among many other sacrifices, the suffragists picketed the White House for one hundred fifty days straight. Many pioneering activists worked for decades on getting women the right to vote and did not see it in their lifetime. Read up on these activists and those from other movements to give you perspective and keep you motivated.

4. **Tell your story.** It makes a difference when sexual assault survivors tell their story. It's really hard to relive the most painful experience in your life, but you put a face on the problem. So if you can—tell your story.

5. **Raise your voice.** People have to keep speaking out. Congress is forced to act when regular people speak out about it. Write, tweet, ask for meetings, call. Take it from a senator: It matters that you continue speaking up and reaching out.

Bonus: Here's one tangible thing to demand. Demand that the Campus Accountability and Safety Act (CASA) gets a vote in the Senate: https://www.gillibrand.senate.gov/campus-sexual-assault.

Under the Obama administration, guidelines were provided by the Department of Education to set a standard for schools, including definitions around consent and strong adjudication policies, because a good number of them didn't have a process for handling sexual assault cases. Those guidelines were recently rolled back by the Trump administration, with the rationale being that the "preponderance of evidence" standard was too hard on defendants. But we don't have a huge problem with defendants not being listened to. We have the opposite problem: survivors not being listened to, not being believed, and facing retaliation.

One of the most important things that CASA mandates is a nationwide anonymous, biennial survey of students. It's needed because administrators don't know what's going on as well as they should. With the survey in place, they'd know if students were underreporting, and they'd know what the climate is really like on campus. And if a school has survey results that say there are assaults, but none are officially reported, parents would know there's a problem. The bill also sets policies and process, including mandating that schools have a confidential advisor, as described previously, available to survivors.

Passing the CASA bill and making its requirements law would be even better than reinstating the rolled-back guidelines.

The bill is bipartisan, with thirty-five cosponsors, including a dozen Republicans. People should demand a vote on the bill. There won't be a vote unless Congress is forced to do it. Urge your congressperson to sign on and to demand a vote.

THE CONSTITUTION
AND FREE SPEECH ON CAMPUS

AND OTHER ISSUES

Freedom of speech is one of the most prized American values. It is protected by the First Amendment. From the birth of our republic until the present, debate over the definition of free speech has remained constant in our public dialogue. Throughout the years, the U.S. Supreme Court has grappled with the parameters of what kinds of words and actions are protected by the Constitution.

THE FIRST AMENDMENT PROTECTS YOUR RIGHT TO

Choose not to salute the American flag and to remain silent. (e.g., taking a knee during the national anthem).
(*West Virginia Board of Education v. Barnette*, 319 U.S. 624. 1943.)

Elect to wear colored armbands to protest a war.
("Students do not shed their constitutional rights at the schoolhouse gate." *Tinker v. Des Moines Independent Community School District*, 393 U.S. 503. 1969.)

FUCK THE DRAFT

Utilize specific "offensive" phrases and words to express a political message.
(*Cohen v. California*, 403 U.S. 15. 1971.)

Use symbolic speech (like burning a flag) as a form of protest.
(*Texas v. Johnson*, 491 U.S. 397. 1989; *United States v. Eichman*, 496 U.S. 310. 1990.)

Donate money to political campaigns (in specific instances).
(*Buckley v. Valeo*, 424 U.S. 1. 1976.)

Advertise products and professional services (with certain limitations).

THE FIRST AMENDMENT DOES NOT PROTECT YOUR RIGHT TO

Make actions for the principal purpose of creating unnecessary panic.
(*Schenck v. United States*, 249 U.S. 47. 1919.)

Set drafts card on fire as a form of protest.
(*United States v. O'Brien*, 391 U.S. 367. 1968.)

Create or distribute obscene materials.
(*Roth v. United States*, 354 U.S. 476. 1957.)

Use obscene speech at a school-sponsored event.
(*Bethel School District #43 v. Fraser*, 478 U.S. 675. 1986.)

Promote illegal drug use at a school-sponsored event.
(*Morse v. Frederick*, U.S. 2007.)

Intentionally incite a crowd (using inflammatory speech) to immediately engage in a violent or illegal action.
(*Brandenburg v. Ohio*, 395 U.S.444)

Publish articles in a school newspaper that your school administration objects to.
(*Hazelwood School District v. Kuhlmeier*, 484 U.S. 260. 1988.)

Privacy on Campus

The Family Educational Rights and Privacy Act (FERPA) is the federal statute for higher-education law and it impacts both student privacy and campus safety. To learn more about your state and federal policies and how these laws might impact your privacy or safety on campus, visit the U.S. Department of Education's site, https://www.ed.gov.

KELLY WICKHAM HURST

FOUNDER, BEING BLACK AT SCHOOL

After spending twenty-three years in the public education system as a teacher, literacy coach, guidance dean, and assistant principal, Kelly Wickham Hurst witnessed firsthand how the system helped white students thrive while continuing to marginalize Black students. As a result, Kelly left the education system and started the organization Being Black at School. We all have a vested interest in a fair school system, and Kelly offers advice on what to look for, what to ask, and how to get information about how the schools in your area are doing when it comes to providing an equitable educational experience for all kids.

The Data Is There

"There are numerous mechanisms for data collection around schools and their students. The Office for Civil Rights has been gathering data for years, noting, for example, how often students are disciplined or rates of bullying. Students of color and students in poverty are disciplined at higher rates than other kids, and this is true all across the country. Black and brown kids with higher incomes do experience better outcomes than those of lower income, so the intersection of race and class is a key factor. When it comes to bullying, LGBTQ students experience the highest rate of being bullied—and therefore, unsurprisingly, also have the top rate of suicide among kids.

"Your local school may not just offer up this kind of data, but the local board of education is responsible for sharing if asked. So ask. If you ask a question and don't like the answer, find out who owns the policy and articulate and escalate your concern to them. If it's a school district policy, take it to the school board. If it's a school policy, take it to the principal."

What Can Teachers and Administrators Do?

"The most important thing school staff can do is investigate their own implicit bias. We all have it; we're not exempt. Don't be bragging on being color-blind. There was a Yale University study of bias in preschool teachers. As one example, they tracked the eye movement of teachers and found their eyes were consistently on Black students, particularly boys. They missed similar behaviors in white students. Given that more than 80 percent of public school teachers are white, but only 49 percent of students are, this is the number-one first step to take."

Kelly's organization, Being Black at School, offers a kit for people who want to start a local chapter in their school district. The starter kit can be found here: https://beingblackatschool.org/bbasxyourcity.

The Tyranny of the "Gifted Track"

"There are many equity issues around the assignment of children to gifted or non-gifted tracks. It's different state by state, and the question to ask is, how is gifted-ness defined and determined? The primary gatekeeper year in most school districts is third grade, when students are just eight or nine years old. And it can often be tied to culture and enrichment activities the child is exposed to outside of school (which can often be tied to the class and income level of the parents).

"What is this giftedness, and is your school system tracking what happens to those on the track and not on the track? For example, if a child can read in kindergarten, some systems identify them as gifted, and yet every child is reading by second grade,

so how much of a child's future is being determined by a relatively short-term advantage? Or in math, a fifth-grade math assessment can bar a child from taking pre-algebra in sixth grade, but that one test and outcome determines the math track they're on for the rest of their primary education, all the way through high school.

"Rather than giftedness being determined at one point in time and remaining static, it should be assessed continuously, at every subject, every grade, every level. It should be fluid, and really good educational systems exist that work like that, but they're rare. It definitely takes more work.

"The problem is that we think third graders aren't smart enough to know about the culling, but they are. They've figured it out, and they figure out that if they're on

WHAT PARENTS CAN DO
Questions to Ask and Policies to Review

- What is the dress code?

- Does the school have any LGBTQ-supporting student alliances? What about safe spaces, and safe bathroom policies for transgender kids?

- How does the school or district take care of student emotional health?

- What are the school or district's restorative justice practices? In other words, how do they respond when kids do things? What are the steps they take before suspension or expulsion?

- What are the percentages of kids who get kicked out for not being prepared for class, or for confrontations in class?

- Does the school/district have a curriculum council? Who is on it?

- What is the police presence in the schools, and who controls that—the school administration, the school board, or is it defined in the local teacher's union contract?

- What kind of training does staff get around implicit bias and cultural competency? What does the state require, and is your district in compliance? Is there a committee? Is it diverse?

"Three million kids attend schools with a police officer, but no guidance counselor."

the non-gifted track, they're targets; they get in more trouble; the teachers care less; and they are penalized more harshly for any mistake. As early as third grade, therefore, Black boys in particular give up on the concept of school and vow to quit.

"There are school systems that don't even know they should be looking at their programs and asking, 'Who is missing? Who is not in the room?' It stems from a belief in the system as a meritocracy, but in my opinion, this kind of tracking is a horrible thing we do, without the data to support it."

School Inequity Doesn't Exist in a Silo

"All of this matters because we can't have conversations about what is happening in schools in a silo. Even within a school district, school boards determine the borders for each school's attendance. It can be a form of educational gerrymandering!

"Here's an example of how inequitable treatment of schools goes far beyond an educational issue. Chicago shut down more than fifty schools to save money in 2013, affecting almost entirely Black and brown students. It caused an increased dropout rate. The question is, can we track and tie that dropout rate to a rise in gun violence? We shouldn't talk about gun violence unless we're willing to talk about other issues—race in transportation, race in housing, race in health care, and yeah, race in schools.

"A sense of history is also important—for example, the number of teachers and administrators who lost jobs post–*Brown v. Board of Education*. Schools closed rather than educate Black kids. Black students in one county in Virginia were out of school for four years! This was less than sixty years ago.

"On the positive side, we know that representation matters in getting better outcomes and policies into schools. Illinois, my home state, has lots of Black representation in its legislature and consequently has passed excellent bills addressing the practice of restorative justice and cultural competency training in our state's schools.

"Knowing all of this, and armed with these questions, anyone can activate at the school level, the school district level, and, ultimately, the local politics level to understand and hopefully improve equity in their local educational system."

HOW TO PUSH BACK ON UNFAIR DRESS CODES

As discipline in schools has become more likely to involve the presence of law enforcement, not just school administration, it has become a hot-button issue. An example of a disciplinary issue that might seem innocuous at first is school dress code. If your school doesn't have a uniform, it's likely to have a documented dress code instead. It may be a code rife with bias. Who cares? Well, from a cultural point of view, biased dress codes reinforce stereotyping, for example perpetuating rape culture or pathologizing hip-hop culture. From a very practical point of view, depending on how your school codifies its dress code and how it handles dress-code violations, biased dress codes can become an early step in the deprioritization of education for girls and in the building of the school-to-prison pipeline for students of color.

WHAT MAKES SCHOOL DRESS CODES BIASED OR UNFAIR?

What is the stated purpose of the dress code? Does it reference "distraction," particularly of male teachers and students? The message of distraction is a message that boys can't be responsible for themselves and that the educational focus on boys is more important than the education of girls.

They can be clearly gendered. Review your school's dress code and see if it specifically (and solely) calls out issues around clothes typically worn by girls, such as visible bra straps and leggings, as well as skirt and shorts length. They may also call out body exposure in a way that is not only gendered but entirely subjective. How much cleavage is too much cleavage? How much skin has to be showing for a shirt to bare too much of a girl's midriff, shoulders, or back? Some dress codes ban visible collarbones! The only common dress-code violation that could be considered more likely to affect boys is the banning of sagging jeans, and that is generally understood to have originated to target boys of color. It's also worth checking if they apply gendered expectations to clothing choices that unfairly target trans students, such as codifying that boys can't wear skirts.

Hair can be politicized. Does your school's dress code call out styles that are very common among African-American students, such as braids, locs, extensions, or even quantifying the appropriate height for hair, therefore banning afros? Does it call out dyed hair, either altogether or just in some of the more bright and "unnatural" colors that are currently popular? Hair dress codes are almost always either racially charged or highly gendered.

Are any dress-code guidelines neutral? There are certainly dress-code guidelines that are less gendered and racialized, although they may still be applied subjectively. Many dress codes ban profane or offensive sayings on T-shirts or sweatshirts. Another example is banning sayings that glorify drug or alcohol use. Where is the line drawn on that? Who decides what's profane and offensive?

What is the discipline approach for dress-code violations? Dress-code violations all too often result in the violator immediately being taken out of class and sent home from school. Blocking a student from the day's education for such infractions is an excessive approach.

HOW TO ADVOCATE FOR CHANGE IN YOUR SCHOOL'S DRESS CODE

Ask for the code in writing. Get the code in writing, and ask how this policy is distributed and communicated to parents, kids, teachers, and administration.

Ask for the enforcement policy around the code. Ask for the guidance given to teachers and administrators around enforcing the dress code. Ask for the discipline process. Do they have guidelines on how teachers may speak to students about dress? Do they have reasonable steps that can be taken before curtailing a student's education?

Ask for statistics. The school or district should have the stats on how the dress code is being applied, and they should be able to provide those stats upon request. Look for what percentage of violators are girls versus boys. What percentage are students of color?

Talk to other parents. Rallying a group to support your efforts is more effective than going it alone. Take what you've learned about the school's dress code and share it with parents, particularly parents of the kids who may be being unfairly targeted or signed out without even knowing it.

Find out who owns the policy and talk to them. You need to know who owns the policy in order to advocate for change effectively. Does this code apply just to your school? Or is it a district-wide policy? If the former, ask why the school has its own policy, and if its individual policy differs from the current district-wide policy (and why). Like any other school policy, the office of the principal is where the buck stops. But if it's a district-wide policy, you need to take it up with the school board. School board meetings are public affairs. Either way, you should be able to have your voice heard directly by the person or people responsible for the policy. Bring your fellow concerned parents when you talk to the school board.

Addressing your school's dress code, particularly the disciplinary process around it, is a good place to figure out how the school operates, how policy and decisions are made, and how it responds to questions and challenges from its parent community. Stand up for girls, for students of color, for trans students, and get *outdated* dress codes *updated*.

The issue of health care has been a political football for decades. No matter who's in office, we need proper care. Here, we share some routes to securing and maintaining your care.

HOW TO FIGHT FOR YOUR REPRODUCTIVE RIGHTS

Women's and non-binary people's bodies have long been a battleground in American politics and culture. In the years following the 2004 March for Women's Lives, attended by more than a million people, emergency contraception became legal to purchase over the counter, reproductive health and rights organizations integrated more inclusive race and gender frameworks, and the Affordable Care Act expanded access to preventive care and contraceptive coverage with no co-pay. Additionally, the United States had in President Obama a pro-choice president for two terms, and in Hillary Rodham Clinton a presidential candidate (and national popular-vote winner) who had famously declared that "women's rights are human rights." But with progress comes backlash, as exhibited by the 2016 election of the anti-choice president Donald Trump and vice president Mike Pence—who has a long track record of enacting extreme anti-abortion laws as governor of the state of Indiana.

In this climate, it is no surprise that the headlines are filled with new threats to reproductive freedom—so much so that advocates across the country have been comparing the state of reproductive rights in America to the famous dystopian book *The Handmaid's Tale* by Margaret Atwood, where women are stripped of their personhood to function solely as vessels for reproduction in a fundamentalist regime. Although abortion has been legal since the landmark *Roe v. Wade* decision in 1973, in January 2017, in Missouri alone, policymakers introduced more than forty bills that would limit women's access to comprehensive health care in their state. And that state is just one example of the upswing of barriers to reproductive justice.

Although we've got our work cut out for us, we still have the power to take care of ourselves and one another, and to raise our voices, making clear to lawmakers that we will not accept a reality where women and non-binary people are forced to carry unintended pregnancies due to a lack of access to critical, safe, and affordable health-care services.

STAY INFORMED

Although attacks on reproductive freedom are hitting us on every level, it's important to stay on top of what's happening. Sign up for text alerts from Planned Parenthood and read news outlets like *Rewire* to hear about the latest news and research impacting reproductive rights and health every day.

LOBBY YOUR ELECTED OFFICIALS

Call, write, and schedule meetings with policymakers. Let your representatives know that your vote depends on their support for reproductive justice.

BECOME A CLINIC DEFENDER

Volunteer to defend clinics and abortion providers by serving as a clinic escort. Call your local Planned Parenthood or women's health center to learn what you can do to help protect women's health and safety.

HIT THE GROUND RUNNING

Canvass and phone bank for your local Planned Parenthood and NARAL affiliates. Look into their outreach teams to volunteer for events, demonstrations, and direct-action campaigns.

STOP STIGMA IN ITS TRACKS

Correct #fakenews and #alternativefacts about reproductive health care. Dispel myths when talking with family members and neighbors by doing your research and setting the record straight in person, via emails, and on social media. Support organizations like the Sea Change Program, a research and development group that promotes cultural change about how we understand, report on, and discuss reproductive health, gender, and sexuality issues.

SHARE YOUR STORY

One in three women has chosen abortion care in her lifetime. Studies show that storytelling about abortion can change hearts and minds and reduce stigma. If you have a story to share about your experience join the 1 in 3 Campaign (www.1in3campaign.org) to share your video or written story. If you're reading headlines in your community about upcoming policy decisions that impact women's health and lives, reach out to your local reproductive rights organizations to see how you might help by writing an op-ed, submitting a letter to the editor, appearing on the local news, or speaking out at a rally.

DONATE

Support your local abortion fund to help ensure that people in need of life-changing support have the resources they need to get safe and legal reproductive care. Contribute to Planned Parenthood, NARAL Pro-Choice America, Groundswell Fund, the Center for Reproductive Rights, the ACLU Reproductive Freedom Project, SisterSong Women of Color Reproductive Justice Collective, or the National Network of Abortion Funds. If your local reproductive rights advocacy organization has a political arm, donate to their action fund or political action committee (PAC) to help them elect officials who support reproductive freedom.

HOW TO GET CONTRACEPTION AFFORDABLY

For the first time in our history, the Affordable Care Act (ACA), established by the Obama administration, made it possible for women to access low-cost birth control. In addition to enabling the majority of our population to plan their families and shape their lives on their terms, the ACA offered 55 million women the means to prevent unintended pregnancy without out-of-pocket costs.

Last year, the American Congress of Obstetricians and Gynecologists reported that the majority of women changed their method of birth control, with almost 15 percent of them motivated by its impact on their wallet.

The impact that the cost of health care has on women, who make less money than men on average, makes affordable access to contraception even more critical. With skyrocketing pharmaceutical costs that put some brands at more than $50 a month, many women are forced to choose between health care, providing for their kids, and putting food on their table.

That's why we have some cost-saving tips to help you decide when and if you want to have a child, chase your dreams, or plan a revolution.

GO TO A FREE OR SLIDING-SCALE CLINIC

Get online. Find your nearest Planned Parenthood clinic by visiting their website and searching for your zip code. Start sleuthing on your local health department's website and research what community health-care centers offer in your city or town.

Use Medicaid. If you qualify for Medicaid coverage, check with your local health department to determine if your state covers over-the-counter emergency contraception and find out what your options are for long-term contraceptive coverage.

PLAY THE LONG GAME

Invest in an IUD. Currently one of the most affordable forms of birth control available, intrauterine devices (IUDs) are increasingly popular. If you want a long-lasting way to prevent pregnancy, a hormonal IUD lasts between three and seven years, and the copper IUD (ParaGard) works for up to twelve years. If you divide the $300 to $400 you may spend over the course of the years you're covered, it is the cheapest method available.

Start an HSA. If you're a planner and your workplace offers a health savings account (HSA) option, set aside the amount you would spend over the course of a year so you can use pre-tax dollars. If you have a high-deductible plan, your HSA account can help support care that would otherwise be out of reach. It can also be used for any contraceptive and prescription costs, including holistic reproductive health-care options. Moreover, funds you put in a pre-tax HSA can be invested for retirement savings if your bank provides that option. Although HSA plans offer many benefits, they have limitations. Be mindful of unexpected costs that exceed what you set aside, tax penalties that result if you withdraw funds that don't qualify (before you are sixty-five), and associated fees that some HSAs charge per transaction or each month.

USE A BARRIER METHOD

Wrap it up. Condoms (including the female condom) are an inexpensive and effective option if you need to save funds. If you aren't having sex frequently, this might be the best fit for you. The added benefit of latex condoms (or non-latex condoms, if you have allergies) is that they protect you from sexually transmitted infections (STIs). If you are considering having sex with someone whose status you're unsure of, having condoms on hand is a good idea no matter what.

COMPARISON SHOP

Pretend you're on *Supermarket Sweep*. If you're a bargain shopper who likes to get a good deal, compare costs between local pharmacies and mail-order companies. While you're searching for these deals by calling or looking online, ask about coupon options.

KEEP IT REAL

Speak up. If your budget is tight, tell your doctor what your budget is and ask for a method that works for you without burning a hole in your wallet. Don't be afraid to ask for free samples or a three-month prescription to maximize savings.

Be authentic, but go generic. Tell your doctor what you're looking for in a pill and ask them to provide non-name-brand alternatives that fit your needs. Don't worry; generic pills are almost identical to the "designer" brands.

Be aware. If you need a non-hormonal method of birth control for medical reasons, track your fertility with the Kindara app to practice the fertility awareness method. Since this approach is not as foolproof as some of the other tools available, use a condom for backup and protection from STIs.

BRI BARNETT

DEVELOPMENT MANAGER, SF LGBT CENTER

Bri Barnett is a lifelong activist and development professional with experience organizing for LGBTQ, labor, environmental, racial, science, and housing justice. She oversees business partnerships and community benefits at the San Francisco LGBT Center. The center is home to the only trans employment program in the nation, which pairs trans and gender nonconforming (GNC) people with jobs.

The lightning-rod issue facing transgender people today is the way they are treated by society and how transphobia manifests itself in our government. Everyday rights cisgender people take for granted—like getting a passport or driver's license, voting, health care, serving in the military, and even getting through airport security—all vary from state to state for transgender people.

Bri has a unique perspective on the needs and challenges of transgender people, for whom the very act of existing is an act of resistance in America's antiquated health-care system.

Health-Care Challenges for Trans People in America

"Unfortunately, the challenges vary wildly based on geography and age. Even in major cities it's not easy for folks to find a gender or LGBT clinic to seek care. People rely on their social networks and online forums to find affirming providers in their area. Sadly, there just aren't health-care providers in the United States willing to treat trans people—many trans folks turn to black- or gray-market sources for hormone replacement therapy (HRT).

"I live in the San Francisco Bay Area, have Kaiser Permanente as my health-care provider, and was referred to Kaiser's Multi-Specialty Transitions clinic. There's a mandatory psychological evaluation and a referral to a doctor specializing in trans health. Pre-surgery, there were mandatory consultations with two psychologists, a medical social worker, a doctor, and then surgeons. Kaiser's process is probably about as close to a 'gold standard' in the nation for streamlined trans care. In California, with proper health insurance, it really can be as easy as going to the doctor, asking for hormones, and going through the official processes."

Bri Barnett believes in raising all boats and leads by example—volunteering with Causa Justa Just Cause and the Transgender Law Center's fundraising departments. She also works with East Bay Meditation Center's Practice in Transformative Action, training others to spread mindfulness in movements for social justice. For more on the SF LGBTQ Center, visit https://www.sfcenter.org/the-center/about.

What Medical Situations Does a Trans Person Encounter That a Cis Person Would Not?

"The 'gold standard' has problems: The gatekeeping is not perfect, as it requires me to prove my identity in a way that cis people seeking plastic surgery don't. And whenever I go outside of the trans clinic, care gets complicated. Nurses drawing blood out of my arm have argued with me about whether or not I should have changed my name. I was misgendered on the operating table as my anesthesiologist was putting me under. While I have not experienced even worse treatment, like denial of care or 'trans broken arm syndrome,' these experiences still make seeking medical care anxiety-provoking."

How Do Trans People Stay Strong and Fight Back?

"Trans folks rely on community and trans-affirming care providers to protect their health and happiness from social stigma and discrimination. Being trans (especially a trans woman in public) means that people are going to threaten, mock, and treat you differently. Facing daily harassment on the street and in the media means that many trans people have a trauma response that can manifest in a variety of symptoms, including depression, anxiety, agoraphobia, and so on. Teaching ourselves remedies like dialectical behavior therapy, cognitive behavioral therapy, and mindfulness helps."

What Sort of Movements and Organizations Are Making Change?

"Given the discrimination that trans folks face, LGBTQ leadership is right to focus on issues like bathroom laws that are fundamentally about trans people's right to exist

DISTURBING STATISTICS
Challenges in Trans Health Care

- 19 percent of trans folks report having been refused care
- 28 percent have delayed seeking medical attention
- 28 percent have been harassed
- 50 percent of trans patients report having to teach their providers about trans health care

STIGMA AND DISCRIMINATION EFFECTS ON TRANS HEALTH

- Substantially higher risk for HIV
- Alarming suicide/depression rates
- Shorter life expectancy
- Increased odds for all of the above for trans folks of color and Black trans women

in public. Campaigns for legal changes and protections have to take place in the court of public opinion. Attitude change is as, if not more, important than enshrining things in law. However, when fighting these laws, national LGBT organizations need to remember to let those most impacted—largely trans women of color—tell their stories to the public so there can be a greater understanding of who we are.

"Continued championing of interpretations of Title IX and Title VII to include gender identity are important to ensure trans access to public life. The ACA (Affordable

"Bathroom laws . . . are fundamentally about trans people's right to exist in public."

Care Act) required trans health care, but too many insurance companies still deny care or don't include trans-competent providers. More advocacy groups should grapple with the reality that many trans folks turn to sex work to survive and incorporate a decriminalization platform into their work.

"Trans people exist at every intersection of society, trans people are immigrants and imprisoned, and we come in every class, color, and creed. Trans people of color have always been at the forefront of our movement. Some of the most impactful organizations work at these intersections. Transgender, Gender Variant, and Intersex Justice Project (TGIJP) not only supports trans people inside and outside of prison, they develop them into movement leaders. Local groups like TGIJP are at the forefront

of the trans movement, but I also have a lot of respect for the Transgender Law Center's work nationally, especially their support of #NotOneMore movement against detention and deportation."

What Happens If Trans Health and Legal Protections End?

"Most trans protections are new. If protections end, trans folks will go back to caring for each other and finding ways to work around the system. There will likely be ally support, where benefactors will offer to take care of trans medical expenses—similar to crowdfunding efforts to help trans folks get passports after the election."

Bri Barnett's Five Tips

What can a transgender person do to protect themselves against a hostile administration?

1. Build a strong, supportive community.

2. Be politically active—get involved in local trans advocacy groups.

3. Know your legal rights.

4. Have a contingency plan to access hormones and other care.

5. Continue to live life however you feel is most appropriate: Be visible while prioritizing safety.

GETTING ACCESS TO DISABILITY SERVICES AND SUPPORT

The Americans with Disabilities Act (ADA) passed in 1990 and was designed to protect the civil rights of people in the United States with both physical and mental disabilities. It is enforced nationwide by the Civil Rights Division of the Department of Justice and is therefore managed at the federal level. In your area, the office for civil rights in your jurisdiction would be responsible for enforcing the ADA. The one exception is employment, which is handled by the U.S. Equal Employment Opportunity Commission (EEOC).

Despite being around for decades, there are still common ways in which the ADA is not properly implemented, whether through ignorance or evasion. Whether you are living with a disability, or you want to be more helpful to others, this guide will itemize the resources that exist to support you, some of the most common violations you may encounter, and specific ways we all can be more mindful about accommodating those with various disabilities in daily life.

GOVERNMENT RESOURCES

https://ada.gov. At this very easy to remember URL, you can find a ton of information about disability-related rights, regulations, and resources. It covers Social Security benefits, housing, employment, education, transportation, accessibility requirements for doing everything from shopping to voting, and more.

Where to complain. You may file a formal complaint with the EEOC via the ADA site. You can file online or you can complain by mail or fax.

Quality-of-life programs. The Administration for Community Living (ACL) is a government agency housed under the Department of Health and Human Services that is dedicated to the concept that older adults and people with disabilities at every age should be able to live where they choose, with whom they choose, and participate in the community. The ACL site is a resource for data and information about programs and grant opportunities, which are available to governments, nonprofits, educational institutions, and even small businesses.

KNOW YOUR RIGHTS: COMMON VIOLATIONS

No grandfathering. Contrary to what you may have heard, older buildings are not exempt or grandfathered in from being accessible. The accessible entrance may not be glamorous, but it has to be there.

No business too small. Small businesses are subject to the ADA. They need at least one parking spot fitting a van with a ramp, and if they offer a customer bathroom, at least one stall must be wheelchair accessible.

Animals allowed. Service dogs are allowed in every establishment open to the public—no papers required.

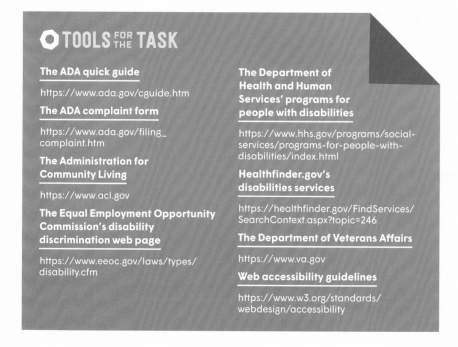

TOOLS FOR THE TASK

The ADA quick guide

https://www.ada.gov/cguide.htm

The ADA complaint form

https://www.ada.gov/filing_complaint.htm

The Administration for Community Living

https://www.acl.gov

The Equal Employment Opportunity Commission's disability discrimination web page

https://www.eeoc.gov/laws/types/disability.cfm

The Department of Health and Human Services' programs for people with disabilities

https://www.hhs.gov/programs/social-services/programs-for-people-with-disabilities/index.html

Healthfinder.gov's disabilities services

https://healthfinder.gov/FindServices/SearchContext.aspx?topic=246

The Department of Veterans Affairs

https://www.va.gov

Web accessibility guidelines

https://www.w3.org/standards/webdesign/accessibility

Make room for wheelchairs. Someone who uses a wheelchair should be able to enter a store and go down its aisles or be able to get to the crosswalk via a curb cut. These are basic accessibility rights, but they are also often avoided due to the cost of retrofitting. Cost is not a valid excuse, according to the law.

Communication assistance. American Sign Language (ASL) interpreters and captioning services (referred to as CART, or Communication Access Realtime Translation) must be provided to individuals who are deaf, hard of hearing, deafblind, or have auditory processing disabilities who request reasonable accommodations. The accommodation provided must meet the individual's communication needs. For example, many deaf people use ASL as their primary mode of communication. In such situations, an ASL interpreter is the appropriate accommodation. However, not all people with hearing loss use ASL, so CART captioning would be the appropriate accommodation. Similarly, people who are blind may request materials in braille or large print, need a guide through a store, or request reading services.

WHAT CAN YOU DO TO SUPPORT PEOPLE WITH DISABILITIES?

Do you plan events? Make sure your venue is accessible—including the exact room or space you'll be using. Restaurants can be technically accessible and yet have private banquet or meeting rooms that are up or down stairs with no alternate access method. Hotels can be accessible, and yet have no way for a speaker to get onstage without climbing stairs. Walk through your event imagining how someone in a wheelchair would manage it. If you produce an event, you must, upon request, provide either a sign-language interpreter or captioning for attendees who are deaf, deafblind, hard of hearing, or who have auditory processing disabilities. While you're at it, provide food options for those who have allergies or dietary restrictions, and make sure food offerings are clearly labeled.

Do you or your company have or run a website or mobile app? Online accessibility is critical, since people with disabilities are just as reliant on the internet as anyone else—and sometimes even more so if physical mobility is an issue. The ADA's web accessibility regulations may not apply beyond government websites, but online accessibility is a best practice for any webmaster, including mobile app developers. The World Wide Web Consortium (W3C) has documented these best practices in great detail.

Do you own or work in a store or restaurant? Keep the aisles clear. Keep sufficient space between tables. One of the most common ADA violations requires no expensive retrofitting; it just requires moving furniture or merchandise around!

Don't forget invisible disabilities. You may feel self-righteous if you see someone get out of a car with a parking permit or walking with their service animal, and they're not in a wheelchair or noticeably blind, but you can't see every disability. Hold your judgment.

Ask before you help someone with a disability. Don't commandeer someone's wheelchair or grab the arm of a blind person, for example. They're used to navigating the world. On a similar note, don't assume you need to speak louder and slower because someone has a disability (unless they ask you to, of course). No, really, it needs to be said!

TAKEAWAYS AND RESOURCES

Tackling big institutions might seem daunting, but do your homework and rally your troops, and you'll be ready to fight the power—policy by policy.

Vet Your Sources

At a time when inaccurate news stories are weaponized by political operatives and foreign governments, stay vigilant about deciphering what news is credible and what is not. You can ensure that the media you're consuming is reliable enough for you to read and even share. Check facts, writing quality, and the credibility and diversity of who's covering the issues. Know the difference between an advertisement and a reported piece. Research whether a particular media outlet promotes a single angle or whether they cover alternate viewpoints.

Follow the Money

Take the time to gain an understanding of who owns the media outlets you read and how it impacts their editorial, staffing, and investment decisions. Doing so will take your media literacy to the next level—and help you garner information for your next media accountability campaign.

Speak Your Mind

Learn and understand the lengths and the limits of protected forms of speech you're entitled to as a citizen, resident, or visitor of the United States. Use your First Amendment rights to create media that changes the conversation and to protect your right to dress in ways that feel comfortable and authentic for you.

Dispel the Objectivity Myth

Own your bias and angle if you're blogging or writing commentary, rather than pretending not to have one. Embrace your unique point of view while maintaining a commitment to credibility, integrity, diverse sources, and fact-checking.

Build What You Need

Whether you're starting a media platform, organizing a new advocacy group, or starting a campaign, build what you and your community need. Don't ask for permission. If you see a gap to be explored, there's your ticket to a new adventure for you and all of the folks you lift up in the process.

Fight for Your Life

You deserve comprehensive and affordable access to health care, reproductive choices, and disability accommodations. It's your birthright, whether current law recognizes it or not. We need you fortified for the fight ahead—so practice self-care and work to protect everyone in our community. When you thrive, we all win!

RESOURCE LINKS

Department of Education Civil Rights Data Collection
https://ocrdata.ed.gov

Other People's Children: Cultural Conflict in the Classroom (Book) by Lisa Delpit
https://thenewpress.com/books/other-peoples-children

Teaching Tolerance Timeline of School Integration in the United States:
https://www.tolerance.org/magazine/spring-2004/brown-v-board-timeline-of-school-integration-in-the-us

The ACLU resource center on the school-to-prison pipeline
https://www.aclu.org/issues/juvenile-justice/school-prison-pipeline

National Center for Education Statistics fast facts
https://nces.ed.gov/fastfacts

Planned Parenthood
https://www.plannedparenthood.org

The Sea Change Program
https://www.seachangeprogram.org

NARAL Pro-Choice America
https://www.prochoiceamerica.org

Groundswell Fund
https://www.groundswellfund.org

ACLU Reproductive Freedom Project
https://www.aclu.org/issues/reproductive-freedom

SisterSong Women of Color Reproductive Justice Collective
sistersong.net

National Network of Abortion Funds
https://abortionfunds.org

Rewire
https://www.rewire.news

Medicaid
https://www.medicaid.gov

Kindara
https://www.kindara.com

National Center for Transgender Equality
https://www.transequality.org/about

American Bar Association on Title VII protections for trans people
https://www.americanbar.org/publications/human_rights_magazine_home/human_rights_vol31_2004/summer2004/irr_hr_summer04_protect-lgbt.html

Veterans Health Administration
https://www.va.gov/health

Acknowledgments

Thanks to our agent, Janis Donnaud, and to Phillip Done for introducing us to Janis!

Thanks to our editor at Ten Speed Press, Patrick Barb.

Thanks to Josh McPhee and Lilli Keinaenen for their amazing artwork.

Thanks to the Ten Speed design and production team members, Kara Plikaitis, Debbie Berne, Emma Campion, and Jane Chinn.

Thanks to the many inspiring advocates, evangelists, activists, organizers, politicians, and doers of good in the world who spoke with us, supported us, taught us, and informed the many disparate pieces of this road map: Amber Goodwin, Amy Ziering, Bobby Jones, Brenton Gieser, Bri Barnett, Carley Knobloch, Chuck Swift, Courtney Macavinta, Craig Newmark, Cristina Tate, Daniel Treiman, David Cohen, Eli Erick, Erica Mauter, Erin Vilardi, Dr. Geoffrey Tabin, Glen Caplin, Guy Kawasaki, Jennifer Pozner, John Boitnott, Joy Johnson, Kate Durkin, Keith Stattenfield, Kelly Wickham Hurst, Senator Kirsten Gillibrand, Lauren Goveo, Laurie Stewart, Lori Luna, Majora Carter, Megan Hunt, Pamela Hadfield, Patrisse Cullors, Paul Ha, Samantha Skey, Sanjay Dave, Sharaine Roberts, Soledad O'Brien, Dr. Tara Sood, Tavi Gevinson.

Thanks to the Ten Speed team who helped bring this book to market: David Hawk and Daniel Wikey.

The authors would like to thank their partners and families for supporting them through this entire process and for being everyday revolutionaries who inspire us. In particular, Carolyn would like to thank Laurent Gerin, Dorothy Mae Giebel, Barry Hughes, and Iris Hough. Elisa would like to thank Chris Page, Monica David, and Gary David. Jamia would like to thank Travis Sullivan, Dr. Willa Freda Campbell-Wilson, and Dr. Johnny Wilson.

Index